ALSO BY DR. BILL THOMAS

What Are Old People For?

Tribes of Eden

Second Wind

Principia

The Good Life

A Fearless Guide to Greater Health and Well-being

Dr. Bill Thomas

Forward by Joel Theisen, BSN

SANA Publishing

Published by Sana Publications
714 N. Aurora St., Ithaca, NY 14850

Thomas, William H.
The Good Life: A Fearless Guide to Greater
Health and Well-being
ISBN 978-1-71659-369-7

Non-Fiction
Aging
Philosophy

The text for this book is set in Verdana
Manufactured in the United States

This book is dedicated to those who spark lives using the magic of questions, conversations, and compassion. Their work makes this world a better place for us all.

Contents

Foreword
by Joel Theisen, BSN

I founded Lifesprk in 2004 because I wanted to empower people to age magnificently. Since then, we have put everything we have — our people, passion, and purpose — into sparking the lives of those we serve. The older people we have worked with over the years have taught us that, just like young people, they have a fierce desire to live life on their terms. We have honored that desire by shifting the focus away from disease and disability, and toward a person-centered approach that actively promotes health, happiness, vitality, and independence.

There is growing concern that healthcare has turned into a fragmented and expensive "sick care" system that does little to prevent illness or improve wellness. We've decided to do something about that. Home is where the heart is, and we believe home is where care belongs. Lifesprk understands there is much more to life than pills and medical appointments. We've developed a technology-enabled, fully integrated, life management approach that puts the person in the center and reduces the need for care provided in facilities and institutions. We are thinking outside the health care box and helping people plan and address important non-medical issues in ways that can prevent visits to the ER, hospitalizations, declining health, and the loss of independence.

We call our alternative the **Lifesprk Experience™ — a whole person approach centered on a customized Life Plan.** The Life Plan relies on seven key elements of well-being, and this book addresses each in turn. Combining robust technology with passionate people and our life management approach creates a seamless experience for seniors and their families. Instead of overwhelming people with a confusing array of choices, Lifesprk offers a single source for the services and supports that people need to keep up with life changes. We love what we do, and our team is always available to provide guidance and support over the phone, through our digital platforms, and in-person.

Lifesprk helps people with medications, appointments, meals, transportation, finances, legal matters, yard work, and household chores. Our skilled medical team helps seniors recover safely at home after a medical procedure or health crisis. We can send a doctor or nurse right to your house if needed or find you the perfect place to call home if your situation and desires change over time. All of this is essential to good health, but there is more to life, so much more. Because we take passion and purpose seriously, we can spark others' lives by inspiring them to be fearless in the pursuit of their purpose and passion.

It is a cruel irony that, while there are more older people on the planet than ever before, we must also contend with an ageist prejudice which holds that every older person's best years are behind them. This is hogwash. Learning, creating, giving to others, reaching for goals, and achieving them are life-long virtues. When we spark lives, we are helping people take hold of the good things in life and enjoy them. The Good Life is available to us at every age. Embracing the good life requires trust, communication, and a fearless commitment to discovering what matters most. Working together, we help people build, or rebuild, the lives they want to live.

That is who Lifesprk is, and this is what we do.

Introduction

This book is about a better way of creating health and wellness. It recognizes that high-quality medical care is essential but cannot, by itself, lead us toward living our best possible life. The time has come to create an alternative delivery system, one based on life experience rather than diseases and diagnoses.

The foundations of America's "sick care" system were laid nearly a century ago. They were designed to serve a much younger population primarily beset by acute illnesses and injuries. Today, chronic diseases affect approximately 133 million Americans, representing more than 40 percent of this country's population. Among people aged 65-74 more than 25 percent live with a disability and this number doubles (49.8 percent) for those over 75.[1] More than ever before, chronic illness and related disabilities define the most critical factors related to health and wellness.

Lifesprk founder Joel Theisen has described a "roller coaster" clinical course that too often defines the experience of older people. An acute episode is treated effectively, but the person's experience with the health care system also leads to a loss of function and reserve capacity. People are routinely discharged from the hospital hungry, sleep-deprived and weakened. These losses increase the risk of another decompensation. When that happens, there is another loss of function. This is the world's most dangerous roller coaster and, for far too many people, the end of the ride results in disability, institutionalization, or death. We can do better than this.

The LEADS model described in this work is the basis for a new approach to the health and well-being of older people. LEADS stands for

- **L**ife
- **E**xperience
- **A**lternative
- **D**elivery
- **S**ystem

Each of these terms deserves a bit of exploration. We use the term "life experience" to describe living the life we want, the life we choose for ourselves. This is what matters most to people. It is possible, for example, to be completely healthy, from a medical point of view, and also completely miserable. No one, not even people who are sick, *wants* medical treatment. No one longs for chemotherapy. Instead, we dream of being healthy, cancer-free and living our lives on our own terms. In order to get off the "roller coaster" described by Theisen, we need to break free from the sick care system and develop a new way of providing services to people who need them. We have to shift the focus away from facilities and institutions and toward homes and communities. LEADS is driven by the idea that, while medical treatment is necessary (and often very effective), it's best used to battle disease -- not as the basis of a life worth living.

The LEADS model combines home and community-based services with seven elements of life, each of which is essential to health and well-being.

Seven Elements

- Belonging -- it's more than just not being alone.

- Health -- it's more than just not taking medicines.

- Home -- it's more than just having a place to sleep.

- Money -- it's more than what's in your pocket.

- Thinking -- it's more than just memories.

- Being -- it's more than just a name and occupation.

- Purpose -- it's more than just a wish.

Why should we care about feeling like we belong? Research has shown a powerful association between loneliness and social isolation and significant negative health consequences which are roughly equivalent to smoking half a pack of cigarettes a day. Lonely people are 50 percent more likely to die prematurely than those with healthy social connections.[2] Other, related, issues are also of major importance. Surveys of older people have long found people place great emphasis on remaining in their own homes as they grow older. One often-cited study found that older people fear the loss of independence more than they fear death. Being able to choose where and how we live our lives is an essential element of health and wellness for most people. LEADS is designed to help people live in the place and manner of their choosing.

What about purpose and passion? The sick-care system is indifferent to the question of life purpose and blind to the restorative power of passion. The LEADS model addresses these questions directly and explicitly. Knowing the answer to the question "Why?" can open up vast new opportunities for health and wellness to flourish, especially in the context of chronic illness.

The LEADS model uses a carefully developed, evidence-based method to guide Life Managers as they work to address the seven elements of well-being. This process uses the following tools to gain greater insight into the whole person and that person's pursuit of health and wellness.

Insight Tools

- **Discover** -- Thoughtful conversations help us identify what matters most to us.

- **Prioritize** -- It is easy to get sidetracked, confused and discouraged if we don't take time to slow down and get clear.

- **Empower** -- Breaking out of an established routine and doing something new takes real effort and it is important to not waste time and energy along the way. There is no substitute for having access to the knowledge and tools that can speed us on our way.

Insight Tools Cont.

- **Ignite** -- When we challenge ourselves to embrace a goal something changes inside of us. Verbalizing a goal puts us "on the record" with the universe.

- **Measure** -- Those who seek growth and improvement over time need to track their progress along the way.

The LEADS model combines these tools with skillful and person-centered exploration of what constitutes one's best possible life. What emerges from these interactions is a Life Plan populated by jointly developed, specific, measurable goals that map a pathway to greater health and well-being. Just as medical treatment plans are constantly revised and improved, we see the Life Plan as a living document which changes over time. Wellness is no accident; it takes thought, partnership, persistence, and tangible measurements to bring it forth.

Each of the following chapters explores an element of the LEADS model in depth and shows readers how to apply its methods to specific health and wellness challenges. The Life Plan and the LEADS model represent a new way of delivering population health at scale. Instead of selecting and focusing on a small slice of clinically complex patients, LEADS allows us to adopt a broader perspective: nearly everyone wishes to be healthy and well and to be able to live their best possible life.

1
The Seven Elements

What Matters Most

We are taught from a young age to treasure youth's virtues. Most people also learn to love, and support, their older relatives. Rarely, if ever, are we encouraged to admire older people, and wish to be like them. Growing old in a society that despises aging can be difficult. This is unfortunate because research on happiness shows that, around the world, growing older brings

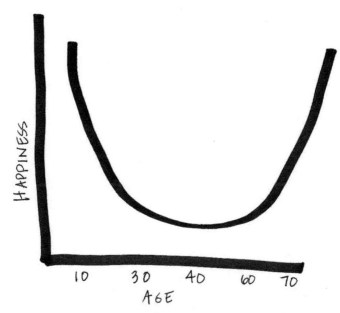

us closer to the life we want to live, and the person we want to be.

The limitations and difficulties associated with aging can also be accompanied by a dawning awareness of one's own mortality. Paradoxically, this insight can also lead to newfound reservoirs of resilience, joy, and satisfaction. Life can certainly get harder as we get older, but it can also get better.

This second coming of age and new lease on happiness is far from automatic. Many older people struggle, especially those who remain attached to the person they used to be and lose sight of the person they can still become. The wife of a world-class athlete relates the story of her husband complaining he can't run as fast or jump as high as he used to. She responded, "It's true you can't but you know what? You're a much nicer person than you used to be." Aging enabled him to be less competitive and more compassionate.

Throughout human history, people have tried to describe the most important elements of a good life. None of these lists have included being able to run fast or jump high, because athletic ability is not among the things that matter most. Love matters. Friendship matters. A giving spirit matters. An understanding of one's own failings and frailty matters. When viewed from the vantage point of age we can see how important the simple things are.

What matters most? Different people will offer different answers but the seven elements listed below offer a good place to start when searching for the good life -- no matter how young or old we may be.

Seven Elements

- **Belonging**
- **Health**
- **Home**
- **Money**
- **Thinking**
- **Being**
- **Purpose**

Belonging-- Meet Helen
it's more than just not being alone

Human beings are social creatures and social connections are vital to our health and well-being at every point in the human lifespan. For most people, the good life is built on a bedrock of family, friends, neighborhood, community, and society. Aging, in particular, is a team sport, and those who age alone can have a very hard time of it.

Helen grew up in a big family with a little house and one bathroom. After she left home she made a family of her own but now she finds herself -- for the first time in her life -- alone. She'll show us just how big a difference social connections can make for someone who is rebuilding a life worth living.

It is important to remember that most older people are pretty healthy and have strong social networks of friends and families. For those who find themselves struggling with social isolation and loneliness, the risks to health and happiness are significant.[3] Studies have linked social isolation and loneliness to an increased risk of heart disease, obesity, anxiety, depression, and Alzheimer's disease. Among people living with heart failure, loneliness quadruples the risk of death and is associated with a 68 percent increased risk of hospitalization, and 57 percent increased risk of emergency department visits.[4]

Helen can make a plan for building connections that can blossom into friendships and help her return to living the good life.

Health -- Meet Bob
it's more than just not taking medicines

Americans tend to equate health with health care which, if you think about it, is backward. Health isn't about a lack of medical diagnoses or the fact that someone doesn't take any medicines. Health and wellness are really about the ability to live life on our own terms, to live where and how we choose.

Access to high-quality health care services is necessary to our well-being, but these, by themselves, can not lead us to true wellness. When we shift our focus from treating illnesses to "what matters most" we begin to see how big the "little things" can be.

When he was a senior, Bob Markuson won the Minnesota High

School high jump crown with a leap of seven feet and one inch. His record still stands today. After graduating he enrolled in community college and set his sights on the 1976 Olympic trials. Then came a motorcycle crash and a badly injured leg. More than 40 years later, he finds himself saddled with a balky knee replacement and struggles to get from his bed to his chair.

Using the MESH (Move, Eat, Sleep, and Heal) framework, Bob can "come back" from his current limitations and hit his goal of walking 10,000 steps a day.

Home -- Meet Alice
it's more than just having a place to sleep

Home is something we understand mainly as a feeling. There isn't, and won't ever be, a single definition for what it means to feel safe, and comfortable, and "at home." For most people though, the feeling of being at home includes being able to (mostly!) do what we want, when we want. Not feeling at home, or being told we can't return home, can lead to depression and a pervasive feeling of helplessness.

Alice knows how it feels to yearn for home. Before her fall, she was living at home with her garden and her cat. She was happy. Now she is living in a nursing home, a pretty good nursing home, as far as the numbers go, but this is not where she wants to be. The question is, after a broken hip, wound infection, a bout of pneumonia, and a significant loss of muscle mass -- can she go home again?

Alice can accept the challenge to build strength, balance, and stamina while her house is being adapted to meet her current needs and once again serve as her home.

Money -- Meet Irene
it's more than what's in your pocket

If forced to choose, most people would likely prefer to talk about sex than talk about money. Conversations about money are both difficult and important. According to the American Psychological Association three-quarters of people surveyed said they had worried about money at some point in the last month. More than a quarter of the people surveyed reported being stressed about financial issues most or all of the time. This anxiety can become acute for people living on fixed incomes who worry their money will "run out" before they die-- leaving them as paupers.

Irene grew up poor but it never bothered her much because, back then, "everybody I knew was poor."

Her mother saw she had a head for numbers and worked hard to put her through college. She graduated, became a CPA, and spent 40 years looking after other people's money. Never married, she lives alone and has started to worry -- about her own finances.

Irene can convert anxiety into action and put together a financial plan which ensures she will always have enough to get by.

Thinking -- Meet Carol
it's more than just memories

A philosopher once claimed, "I think, therefore I exist!" Our ability to think for ourselves is central to our existence and people fear dementia precisely because they fear they will cease to exist as a person as their memory fades. If I can't think clearly -- will I still be me? A National Institute on Aging study, which has tracked a thousand men and women since 1958 to observe changes associated with aging, found concerns about declining sexual interest and personality changes, among other things, but memory loss emerged as what people worry about most.

Carol was blessed with a long and happy marriage to a kind man named Floyd Merrick, Jr.. After Floyd got lost while walking the dog, she arranged an appointment with their primary care provider. On the followup visit, Floyd was told he had Alzheimer's disease. Floyd took the news pretty well, all things considered. Carol saw the diagnosis as a catastrophic end to what had been a happy life with the man she loved. Her life quickly began to unravel.

When a diagnosis of dementia is made, most of the attention is directed to the person receiving the diagnosis. After all, this is a terminal diagnosis. The truth is that dementia impacts the entire family and spouses, in particular, experience a tremendous and immediate impact on their thinking, their emotions, and their understanding of what role they are to play in the marriage.

Carol can reimagine her life and adapt to being married to a person living with dementia. The good life is available to her if she knows where to find it.

Being -- Meet Floyd
it's more than just a name and occupation

It takes a long time to figure things out. Most people experience decades of trial and error before they can complete the phrase "I am..." with confidence, and the longer we live, the more answers we find. Humans are remarkably long-lived creatures and when we look back on our lives we can see them as a succession of chapters joined end to end. If we are lucky, those chapters form an extraordinary story of love and becoming, a whole much greater than the sum of its parts.

In the case of Floyd Merrick Jr., there were chapters about growing up on a dairy farm. There was a stint of military service (he is a former

Marine), and a long chapter of happy marriage to Carol, the love of his life. Now comes the chapter of living with Alzheimer's. He knows there is no cure for Alzheimer's and wants to be ready for the last chapter of his life when it comes.

Floyd, Carol, and their daughter Kate can share some difficult and loving conversations about the end of life and complete the documents they need to ensure that their wishes are respected as the end of their lives draw near. As Floyd says, "I'm going to tell it like it is and not waste the time worrying about things I don't need to be worrying about." Choosing how we want to die says much about how we want to live.

Purpose -- Meet Tom
it's more than just a wish

Does having a purpose matter? A JAMA study published in 2019 showed that, among people over the age of 50, having a strong life purpose leads to improvements in both physical and mental health and enhances overall quality of life.[5] A survey of U.S. military veterans revealed a connection between purpose and greater resilience. A strong sense of purpose was also correlated with improved recovery from PTSD.[6] Whatever our life experience may be, connecting to purpose can help us answer the question: "Why am I here?"

Tom left his right arm in Vietnam. Drafted into the Army straight out of high school in '69, he shipped out in '70. A land mine killed two of his buddies and shattered his arm

on August 8 of that year. He was
choppered out and the surgeons amputated just below the shoulder. After
the Army, he became the "best one-
armed forklift operator you ever saw."
Now, he's a widower, alone in his recliner, in front of a TV that never stops
reminding him that American boys are
still out there, still losing their lives
and limbs in faraway lands.

We grow up understanding that
life requires constant change but
then, somehow, in the later years
of life many people lose track of the
importance, and value, of change.
The most powerful tool for change?
Purpose. Tom can accept the challenge
to connect to and act on what matters
most to him.

2
Building a Life Plan

The Power of Planning

Let's imagine an airline, we'll call it "Up in the Air" (UITA), and it's running ads in your city. The spots feature friendly and smiling people, glorious aerial shots, and a compelling tagline: "Take-Off for Adventure!"

Hmmm, you think, "I could use an adventure," so you call the number on the screen...

UITA: Up in the Air how can we help you?

You: I'm ready for an adventure!

UITA: Great, where do you want to go?

You: Well that's the thing, I don't know for sure.

UITA: Perfect! Who will you be traveling with?

You: I just saw your ad and picked up the phone, so I don't know, maybe I'll go alone, or maybe I'll take a friend.

UITA: Also not a problem! So why are you looking for adventure?

You: Your ad was so nice and I thought, wow, I could really use something new in my life.

UITA: Yes, we do make very nice ads.

You: But I guess I'm not sure why; I haven't really thought about it.

UITA: Your total will be $1,365.75. How would you like to pay?

You: Pay? How can you charge me when I don't even know where I want to go?

UITA: This is Up in the Air; we don't actually fly airplanes. We sell tickets to people like you. You know, people with no plan, no idea where they are going.

You: Come on! That's ridiculous.

UITA: Many people say that but our business is booming. People without a plan can go anywhere, or nowhere; it really doesn't make a difference. We just cut out the planes, the pilots, the fuel, and the food, in order to save you money.

You: Well, you're not getting my money.

UITA: I understand, sir, but if you had a plan you would have called one of those other airlines; you know, the ones with the planes.

You: Well, I'm not giving you money just so I can go nowhere.

UITA: As you wish, but don't ever hesitate to call us back. We're here 24/7 and...

Click.

You: Insane. That's just insane!*

*Life never works out like you planned but having no plan is no way to live a life.

Discover
Thoughtful conversations help us identify what matters most to us.

We make plans because we sense a gap between the way things are and the way we want them to be. Something's not right and we feel a need to make things better. It turns out, however, that figuring out what's wrong is much harder than it seems. This process requires us to make a decisive shift from a feeling to a certainty. What, exactly, is it that needs fixing? How confident are we that what we wish for is what we really need, or even want?

When we need facts, we know where to look. Whether we seek answers online, or in person, we can be confident that, somewhere out there, there is a trustworthy source of information who can tell us who won the Oscar for Best Director in 1938.[7] When it comes to our own emotions, our hopes, our dreams, and our fears, however, there is no external authority with the answers we need. **When we look inward, we often find that conversation is the best search-light.**

The formal definition of "conversation" is "a talk, especially an informal one, between two or more people, in which news and ideas are exchanged." The best conversations are friendly and go wherever the interests of the conversationalists take them. The worst conversations are one-sided, boring, and involve one person trying to get something from the other. The opportunity to talk with someone about life and the lives we are living is a gift of great value. We honor this gift by opening ourselves to the act of discovery. What we hear matters much more than what we say.

The act of conversational discovery makes use of thoughtful,
open-ended inquiries.

As we learn more about another
person we begin to understand why
they feel the way they do. We can
also help them decide what matters
most to them. We get only one life so
it makes sense to have a plan for that
life. Creating a Life Plan can add more
years to your life and, as the saying
goes, more life to your years.

Life Plan Discovery Questions:

- If you could spend time with anyone, who would you choose to be with?

- Are you getting the rest you need?

- Are you living the way you want to live?

- Do you feel like you have enough money?

- Are you worried about your memory?

- What did your mom say was the best thing about you?

- What gets you out of bed in the morning?

Prioritize

It is easy to get sidetracked, confused and discouraged if we don't take time to slow down and get clear.

Learning to prioritize is essential to making a useful plan because just putting together a laundry list of goals leads to confusion and a lack of focus. A laundry list? Who makes a list of their laundry? People living in 19th century America made laundry lists, that's who.

The first commercial laundries appeared in the1860's and they required customers to make a list of the items they were dropping off so the right dresses and suits could be returned to the right people. A notice from the March 4, 1871 edition of the Pacific Commercial Advertiser tells the tale:

"Mr. W. M. Wallace has got up a very neat and convenient card for laundry lists, which on examination will at once strike one as useful as well as novel. The different articles of clothing sent to the wash are by an ingenious arrangement numbered each under its separate head, without the bother of writing or making figures. There are separate lists for ladies, gentlemen, and families, and every ordinary article of clothing that requires washing has its separate place, from one piece up to twelve. We are confident that on trial it will be found of indispensable use in every household, and a valuable source of economy."

Now, where were we?

Oh! Right! Prioritization!

It is easy to get sidetracked, confused and discouraged if we don't take time to slow down and get clear. Fortunately, there is a method for examining and ranking the kinds of goals that make Life Plans work. The SMART method, originally developed by Peter Drucker, helps us evaluate multiple goals using consistent criteria.

SMART goals are:

- Specific,
- Measurable,
- Actionable,
- Realistic, and
- Time-bound

As we will see, each of these factors can be rated on a scale of 1 to 5. We can use the idea of specificity to show how this works.

Specific

1 - The goal lacks any specificity.
(I want happiness.)

2 - The goal is vague.
(I want to feel happier.)

3 - The goal has some specificity.
(I want to feel better about my
body.)

4 - The goal is specific.
(I want to get into shape so I can feel
better about my body.)

5 - The goal is highly specific.
(I want to develop my upper body
strength and muscle tone so that I like
the way I look when I wear sleeveless
tops.)

This approach is applied in a
similar fashion to assess each goal's

measurability, actionability, realism, and time boundedness. This system simplifies and clarifies the task of choosing where to place our focus. If everyone used the SMART system to rank their life goals -- "Up in the Air" would soon be out of business.

Empower

Breaking out of an established routine and doing something new takes real effort and it is important to not waste time and energy along the way. There is no substitute for having access to the knowledge and tools that can speed us on our way.

After we accept the challenge of reaching a goal we need to prepare for the journey ahead. Established routines are hard to change and it is important that we waste as little time and energy as possible as we work toward a goal. Fortunately, researchers have been looking carefully at the process of change and we now understand how important it is to prepare and equip ourselves for the journey. *Knowledge* helps us understand the change we seek while having the right *tools* equips us for the work which lies before us.

The types of knowledge we are interested in can be sorted into three categories. There are also three kinds of tools that can equip us for new ways of living.

Three Types of Knowledge

1. Personal Knowledge comes from what we learn through direct experience. The struggle to solve the problems of everyday life can teach us much if we are willing to pay attention.

2. Procedural Knowledge comes with the ability to successfully perform a skill. Learning new skills is a lifelong endeavor and is especially important for older people.

3. Propositional Knowledge relates to the possession of relevant facts. An expanded fund of knowledge allows us to make better decisions. For example, many people living with chronic illness improve their health and well-being by developing a deep understanding of their particular conditions.

Tools for New Ways of Living

1. Mechanical Devices help us do new things. One of the simplest inventions has also had the biggest impact on the lives of older people. Eyeglasses were invented in 1275 and they have enabled billions of elders to live fuller, more active, lives.

2. Digital Devices help us communicate in new ways. The idea that older people can't or won't embrace new technology is a damaging myth. In fact, older people have significant experience mastering new technology; they grew up with tube radios and now carry smartphones.

3. Social Practices help support new behaviors. There is a saying that when you want to go fast -- go alone. When you want to go far

> -- travel with others. Aging is a team sport and we want to go far, not fast. How we connect to and collaborate with other people has a major impact on how satisfied we are with our lives.

A Life Plan that doesn't explore and exploit knowledge and tools is like an airline without pilots or planes - it won't take you anywhere.

Ignite

When we challenge ourselves to embrace a goal something changes inside of us. Hidden things, thoughts we had not spoken aloud, are brought into the open. The act of stating a goal puts us "on the record" with the universe. This is actually a big deal in itself, but this process can ignite even greater change, if we remain open to this possibility. Accepting a challenge and then preparing and equipping ourselves to meet that challenge very often leads to another challenge, and another goal, and another effort to learn, master new skills, and change our lives for the better.

Experts in the subject of breaking and making habits are clear on this point. Most bad habits grow in the soil of stress and boredom. The antidote to stress and boredom is action. Picking a goal and working toward it has been shown to reduce negative emotions and foster positive feelings. It is easier to create and sustain change if we remember that the ideas and inspirations that got us started may not be the ideas and inspirations that keep us going. As we change we need new tools and new information. We use a spark to start a fire and then -- we need to feed the fire. New challenges feed the fire better than anything else.

Measure

Many people remember the game "pin the tail on the donkey." It was fun and funny (or it seemed fun and funny at the time) because the blindfold made it hard to do the task correctly. If you can't see what you are doing, you're likely to end up with a donkey with a tail pinned to his nose. When we get a bit older we start to realize that "flying blind" is no way to go through life. Building a Life Plan without including useful measurements...well, let's just say, it's a bad idea. When we seek growth and improvement over time we must track progress along the way.

The "Up In The Air" airline has no use for maps, weather reports, or flight plans because they don't take anyone anywhere. Numbers mean nothing to people without a plan. For the rest of us, measurements are crucial to helping us get where we are going as quickly and safely as possible. Plans and numbers are linked together by goals and, as we have seen, it's best when those goals are SMART (specific, measurable, attainable, realistic, and time-bound).

Irene uses a scale designed to assess anxiety to help her put her financial worries behind her.

Bob uses a fitness tracker to guide him on his journey to 10,000 steps a day.

For Alice, measurements of her functional capacity are central to her effort to "go home again."

Helen's progress toward a greater sense of belonging is monitored by a simple three-question quiz developed by the Campaign to End Loneliness.

Carol's journey into providing care for a person living with dementia can be evaluated, in part, by using a test that measures caregiver stress.

Tom's new life as a philanthropist is accounted for by the dollars he has raised to support a cause he is passionate about.

In the end, measurements are essential to discovery; they inform us about the difference between what we suppose to be true and what is, in fact, true. This is the most important difference of all.

Life doesn't make any sense
without interdependence. We
need each other, and the sooner
we learn that the better for us all.

-- Joan Erickson

3
Belonging

Discover

Solitude is the pleasure that comes when we want to be by ourselves and find time to be alone. Loneliness is the pain we feel when we wish for companionship but have none. It is important to distinguish between these two, very different, states of being because studies have shown that loneliness has a health impact similar to smoking 15 cigarettes a day and increases the risk of premature death by 30 percent.[8] Many of us assume people who are single or living alone are the most at risk for loneliness but studies have shown high levels of social isolation among older

people who are married, with especially high rates among those who are
functioning as caregivers.[9]

Health care professionals
measure vital signs because they
are just that -- vital. When we shift
our focus from sickness to health it
becomes obvious that understanding
a person's social connections is vital.
Doing this in a skillful manner requires
us to plunge into the domain of
interpersonal relationships. These connections define the circles of concern
within which we live. Because of the
stigma surrounding loneliness, simply
asking, "Do you feel lonely?" may
not be the best way to gain insight.
The following questions may be more
useful.

Belonging Discovery Questions:

- **If you could be with anyone, who would you choose to be with?**

- **Who do you worry about?**

- **Who worries about you?**

- **Who do you miss the most?**

Most older people are actually pretty happy with their networks of friends and relatives. The experience of those struggling with loneliness, however, varies widely. As we learn more about a person who is contending with social isolation we can begin to determine whether the problem is acute or chronic, mild or serious. We can get the information we need using conversation and gently probing questions.

Prioritize

Helen's Story

I grew up in a big family. I was the youngest of six and nobody had their own room. Dad worked at the mill and Mom worked at home taking care of us and teaching piano lessons after school. I met Joe, my husband, in elementary school and we were high school sweethearts. We have three children. My oldest, Danny, was born when I was 20, then came Katie and Ricky. Ricky died in a car accident; a drunk driver ran a red light. Ricky was on his way home from a varsity basketball game; it was the first time we let him take the car at night. I worked in the high school as a secretary back then. That was a really hard time for all of us. Danny turned 60 this year. My goodness, that is hard to believe. He's retired from the police department up in Fresno. He calls me on Sundays. Katie married a very nice man from Spain. They live in Barcelona. I visited them a couple of years ago -- after Joe died. Now it's just me rattling around in this old house. I never thought I would be alone, like this.

☼

Health care professionals are skilled at prioritizing clinical conditions and setting goals accordingly. We can do the same with the Seven Elements of Well-Being. With respect to social isolation, we can think about its intensity and duration.

Social Isolation	Acute	Chronic
Mild	Simple/ Short-Term	Simple/ Long-Term
Serious	Complex/ Short-Term	Complex/ Long-Term

Unlike clinical goals, which are derived from clinical research, Life Experience goals are centered on people. What do they want? What do they need? How can we help them be more connected in ways that are meaningful to them? As we think about Helen's story, we can begin to imagine some of the goals for belonging that might be helpful.

Potential Goals:

A: Move in with Danny and his wife.

B: Return to Barcelona for an extended visit with Katie and her husband.

C: Begin weekly volunteering at the high school where she once worked.

D: Start a local chapter of Mothers Against Drunk Driving.

SMART Scoring

(1 is the lowest score and 5 is the highest score)

Goal List	A	B	C	D
Specific	3	4	5	4
Measurable	2	3	4	4
Actionable	2	2	4	2
Realistic	2	2	4	2
Time-Bound	3	3	5	2
Total	12	14	22	14

The initial SMART scoring suggests volunteering at the high school would be a good place to start.

Helen has accepted the challenge to volunteer 10 hours a week at the high school for the next year with a total goal of 500 hours.

Empower

No one is going to "empower" Helen to do anything. **People are the source of their own growth and development as well as the willingness to change and the perseverance needed to reach the goal they have set for themselves.** That being said, when we are sick it really is helpful to have a skilled doctor available to guide us on our healing journey. The same is true when we create an intention to change our lives for the better. A coach, mentor, friend, or ally who can help us empower ourselves has a unique value.

As for Helen, she has accepted the challenge to launch a new career as a high school volunteer. This is harder than it sounds and she will need access to new knowledge and tools if she is going to succeed.

Empowering Belonging Questions:

- What kind of direct experiences could prepare her for a challenge of this magnitude?

- What new skills should she develop?

- Much has changed in the years since she worked there-- what does she need to know? Are there tools that would be helpful to her?

- Should she upgrade to a smartphone?

- How can her role as a volunteer help her expand her social circle in other ways?

While Helen can find the answers to all these questions all by herself, her odds of success rise dramatically when she is able to share the journey with someone who is knowledgeable, experienced, and invested in her success.

Ignite

We count down before we launch a rocket. "5, 4, 3, 2, 1, Ignition, Lift-Off!" This marks the beginning of the journey. The same is true with Helen's new adventure as a high school volunteer. As her work evolves, there will be opportunities to spark new goals and further adventures.

Helen's New Story

Well, to be quite honest, it scared me half to death at first. I thought to myself what do I know about kids these days? But, you know, kids are kids. You should see the way they dress, I never would have allowed it, but times change. Mainly kids today are just like my kids were, just like how I was when I was their age. They really just want someone to talk to, someone who will listen to them. I'm a good listener. Not long after I started my macular degeneration got worse and I thought that's it, I'm done. I couldn't drive anymore. But the kids helped me put an app on my phone that lets me call a car right to my house. I call another car when I want to go home. The drivers are all different and they are very interesting people! The art teacher found out I used to have a potter's wheel and a kiln and now she has me helping out in her classroom. I've even thrown a few pots of my own. The kids all call me Helen, instead of Mrs. Whitmore. I like that. I'm Helen and I listen to kids!

☼

A proverb about mountains is relevant to Helen's journey. "The higher we climb, the farther we can see." Helen has climbed up and out of a pit of loneliness and, in doing so, expanded her vision. As her ambitions grow, she'll continue to benefit from access to new knowledge and tools. This is how a spark becomes a flame that warms hearts and changes lives.

Measure

Measuring social isolation and loneliness is challenging for two reasons. First, admitting to loneliness carries a stigma and many people are reluctant to admit to this type of suffering. Second, our ageist society expects older people to be lonely; after all, they're old. **The truth is-- aging does not cause loneliness.**

As Helen told her story we could begin to see how heavily social isolation and, more to the point, loneliness was weighing on her. As we learned more about her we were able to help her develop some possible goals. Then we showed her how to use the SMART evaluation grid to analyze those goals and pick one with a specific, measurable, attainable, goal with a timeline. Now, what about those measurements?

Addressing specific issues around loneliness is an important part of our approach to health and wellbeing. As we help people expand their social networks we can measure the impact on their life experience. The United Kingdom's "Campaign to End Loneliness" (CEL 2015) tool has just three statements and is incredibly easy to use.[10][11]

Loneliness Measure

- I am content with my friendships and relationships.
- I have enough people I feel comfortable asking for help at any time.
- My relationships are as satisfying as I would want them to be.

To each of these statements, respond with one of the following answers:

Strongly disagree-- 4
Disagree-- 3
Neutral-- 2
Agree-- 1
Strongly agree-- 0

Total the scores for all three questions. This gives a possible range of scores from 0 (least lonely) to 12 (most lonely).

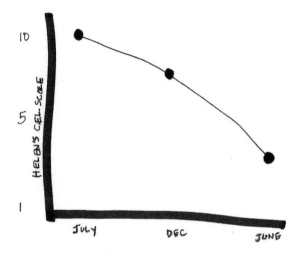

When Helen started this journey her CEL score was 10. After a year of volunteering her score improved to 3. This is a big change. She also tracked her volunteering hours for the year. Drumroll, please! She clocked 576 hours at the high school. She is now able to do video calls with her son and daughter weekly. We have proof that she is less lonely and we can see how her social engagement is improving her life and the lives of others.

This is the power of a Life Plan.

"It is the sweet, simple things of life
which are the real ones after all."

-- Laura Ingalls Wilder

4
Health

Discover

With age comes an elevated risk of chronic disease. Approximately 80 percent of older adults have at least one chronic disease, and 77 percent have at least two. Chronic conditions account for 75 percent of the money our nation spends on health care, yet only one percent of health dollars are spent on public efforts to improve overall health.[12] [13] The Life Experience Alternative Delivery System (LEADS) can address this imbalance by expanding our focus from medical conditions to the bigger question of how we experience our lives.

Is there a difference between how we are living and how we wish we were living? Is the difference large or small? What would it take for us to be able to live our best life possible? These questions lie at the heart of discovery.

Move, Eat, Sleep, and Heal

The professions of medicine and nursing are powerful and when used skillfully, capable of extraordinary feats. Our focus on life experience represents an important addition to what traditional health care can accomplish. The "MESH" concept reminds us we need to "Move," "Eat," "Sleep," and "Heal." Based on published research that validates the value of these elements of daily life, MESH leads us to ask simple questions.

Health Discovery Questions

- **How many steps do you think you take in a typical day?**

- **How often do you eat breakfast?**

- **How much sleep do you get during a typical night?**

- **How do you typically feel about your health?**

When working with people to set MESH goals it is important to remember this work isn't about fitness, or nutrition, it's about daily life. The goal isn't to join a gym or become a vegan (although it is fine if this is what some of us want to do); the goal is to help mesh MESH with daily life. MESH is about making small changes that, over time, add up to greater health and well-being.

Move

Researchers from Walking Behavior Laboratory have developed an index that quantifies exercise levels in healthy adults:[14]
- Sedentary: Less than 5,000 steps/day
- Low Activity: 5,000 to 7,499 steps/day
- Somewhat Active: 7,500-9,999 steps/day
- Active: 10,000 steps/day
- Highly Active: More than 12,500 steps/day

They also found that healthy older adults average 2,000-9,000 steps per day and people living with a disability or a chronic illness average about 1,200-8,800 steps per day. Both groups can benefit from a more physically active lifestyle and one of the easiest ways of doing that is by walking more. The researchers found that just using a pedometer led to an average increase of approximately 775 steps per day and 2,215 steps per day in the two groups respectively.

Eat

Eating well is an important part of being well. Sometimes, the best place to start a conversation about food is to talk about breakfast. A wide range of studies show how breakfast can form the foundation of a healthy diet. Some of the advantages of eating breakfast include:[15]

- Maintaining a healthier weight
- Consuming less fat throughout the day
- More likely to meet fruit and vegetable consumption goals
- A higher daily calcium intake
- A higher daily fiber intake
- Improved memory and attention

LEADS can lead people toward greater health and wellness with a focus on simple things that fit into the rhythm of daily life and have been shown to make a difference. These small successes are the foundation on which even more important changes in habits and routines can be built. Talking about breakfast might seem silly but it can help us explore common ground and open the door to deeper understanding.

Sleep

An abundance of evidence shows that sleep deprivation is bad for the brain. We know, for example, that medical interns make substantially more serious medical errors when they work frequent shifts of 24 hours or more than when they work shorter shifts.[16] On the flip side, getting enough shut-eye can help us think more clearly and solve problems more

effectively.[17] Good sleep also contrib-
utes to good health. According to Dr.
Michael Twery, a sleep expert at NIH,
"Sleep affects almost every tissue
in our bodies; it affects growth and
stress hormones, our immune system,
appetite, breathing, blood pressure,
and cardiovascular health."[18]

Older people often struggle
with poor sleep hygiene. **The word
"hygiene" refers to healthy habits
and we can cultivate healthy sleep
habits as well as good handwash-
ing habits.** For example, complaints
about impaired sleep may actually
relate to misunderstandings about
how sleep changes as we age. Normal
aging results in increased sleep
fragmentation. This is a fancy way of
saying it is normal to wake up more
frequently during the night as we grow
older. Increased sleep fragmentation
is also associated with decreased
sleep efficiency. A 100 percent sleep

efficiency rate would mean we fall asleep instantly when we lie down and sleep through the night. Growing older naturally reduces sleep efficiency. These changes are best managed by introducing new habits and expectations.

Sleep Hygiene

- Create a regular sleep cycle using the same bedtime and wake up time, even on the weekends.
- Create a relaxing bedtime ritual with at least an hour away from screens and bright lights before retiring.
- How much you move is related to how well you sleep. Vigorous exercise is best, but even light exercise is better than no activity.
- Your bedroom should be cool (between 60 and 67 degrees), quiet and dark. Consider using blackout curtains, eye shades,

earplugs, "white noise" machines, humidifiers, fans and other devices to create a good environment for sleep.
- Avoid bright light in the evening and expose yourself to sunlight in the morning. This will keep your circadian rhythms in check.
- Using your bed only for sleep and sex can strengthen the association between bed and sleep and comfort.

Heal

This is the most personal of the MESH factors. Our culture sends powerful messages equating healing with a "return to the way things used to be." Sometimes this is accurate. We can break an arm and, if we get good care, it can be, as Hemingway said, "stronger at the broken places." As we age, however, our focus begins to shift from acute to chronic conditions. As we collect these diagnoses it starts to become clear that we cannot go back to the way things used to be. Some people react to this insight by seeking medical treatment from a wide variety of professionals and taking a very large (and unhealthy) number of medications. They do this because they want their lives to go back to the way they used to be. But that's impossible.

We can help ourselves and others heal by illuminating the power of looking forward and seeking out a new normal. No, we cannot make Diabetes, or Dementia, or COPD go away. Yes, we can help people live with these conditions in ways that lead to health and happiness. The power of this insight can be seen in the shift away from the language of suffering and victimization. "She suffers from..." "He is a... victim." We now speak of people "living with" certain chronic conditions.

"A person living with..." This re-framing has great power because it puts the person first, it uses "living" as a verb, and it puts the disease last -- where it belongs.

Life is full of changes and we can thrive by continuing to find a new normal. Learning how to live with chronic conditions opens the door to greater health and well-being and reduces the suffering resulting from the false equation of health with the absence of disease.

Prioritize

Bob's Story

When he was a senior, Bob Markuson won the Minnesota High School high jump crown with a leap of seven feet and one inch. His record still stands today. After graduating he enrolled in community college and set his sights on the 1976 Olympic trials. Then came a motorcycle crash that badly injured his right leg-- his jumping leg. After a year of physical therapy he tried jumping again. "I just couldn't do it. My leg just wasn't the same," he recalls. The fact that his high jumping career was over sent Bob's life into a tailspin. "It took me a while to pull myself out of it. It took years, about eight years."

In time, he finished college and launched a career. In 2015 he and John got married but, even as his life was getting better, his knee kept getting worse. The pain was, mostly, bearable and he coached high school high jumpers while working for 3M. A couple of years ago it got to be too much and he gave up on coaching and retired from work. "I had to use a cane to get around and I could hardly sleep at night. I was miserable." An orthopedic surgeon replaced his knee and Bob hoped the pain would end there. But it didn't. He became dependent on oxycontin, gained a lot of weight, and stopped going to physical therapy. Things got bad.

Then, things started getting better.

Potential Goals

A: Get better sleep at night.

B: Lose 20 pounds.

C: Compete in the Senior Olympics High Jump

D: Be able to walk 10,000 steps a day by summer

SMART Scoring

Goal List	A	B	C	D
Specific	3	5	4	4
Measurable	2	3	3	5
Actionable	3	3	1	3
Realistic	2	3	1	3
Time-Bound	1	1	4	4
Total	11	15	13	19

Bob set a goal: I want to be able to walk 10,000 steps a day before Independence Day.

Empower

Bob has a lifelong interest in athletics and has competed at an elite level in track and field so it might seem like there would be little new personal knowledge that would be useful to him. Wrong! While he does have a lifetime of experience with athletic competition Bob's only experience with recovery from injury came decades ago and, by his own account, did not go well. "It took about eight years to pull my life together." Bob can benefit from direct experiences that give him greater insight into how rehabilitation differs from competition. This is not about returning to championship glory, it's about finding a new normal suited to his current age, abilities, and interests.

Learning to live with a titanium knee requires people to develop new skills, new ways of moving, new ways of using their bodies. The first round of rehab did not yield the best results but a person who wants to walk 10,000 steps a day has a reason to try again. It will be important for Bob's next physical therapist to know about his goal and tailor the program to meet the challenge. Unfortunately, there is a tendency for older people to embrace ageist beliefs such as "I'm over the hill." or "You can't teach an old dog new tricks." We can counter these beliefs with facts about aging. For example, research has shown that, all over the world, the 70's are the happiest decade of life. Bob is in his late 60's so, for him, the best may be yet to come.

Mobility aids (canes, walkers, wheelchairs) have long been stigmatized but it is possible to reframe these aids as tools for building strength and independence. An athlete like Bob has an abundance of experience with training gear and it is good to position needed devices in that light. There are a plethora of fitness trackers and it would be worthwhile to work with Bob on selecting the device that best suits his style. Used regularly, these devices generate performance data Bob can use to track his progress toward 10,000 steps. Trackers can also be used to create online communities of people who are working toward greater fitness, less pain, and more freedom. Aging is a team sport after all.

Ignite

Bob's New Story

When I started all this I weighed 226 pounds and walked an average of 218 steps a day. More pounds than steps! It really blew my mind when I saw those numbers. My resting heart rate was 84. Now it's 62. What can I say, I like numbers. My right knee went from 71 degrees extension to 100 degrees. Anyway, I met my 10,000 steps goal in mid-June and just kept going. The trackers helped but the MESH idea really pulled it together for me. Everything is connected. When I started moving more it hurt like hell but pretty soon I was getting tired enough that I looked forward to going to bed at night. Like they say, "the motion is the lotion" and the pain at night eased off quite a bit and I slept better. My tracker gives me a bunch of sleep data but I really don't know what to make of it. I can read a bathroom scale though and I'm down to 194 pounds. I could afford to lose a few more pounds. Diet was never a big thing when I was competing; we just ate whatever we wanted, but now I am all about paying attention to what I am eating. Slow and steady weight loss, that's the thing.

Track and Field practice starts in March around here and I will be back in coaching. There's a girl on the team I think could be a state champion -- she just needs a good coach. I get that. A good coach can make a big difference.

By starting with a tight focus on a specific, achievable goal we can build momentum toward other parts of the MESH model. More exercise yields less pain and more sleep. A better diet delivers more energy and healing capacity. A commitment to finding one's new normal can take the place of a painful longing for the way things used to be. One good thing can lead to another. This is the power of a well-conceived, well-executed, Life Plan.

Measure

Sports are a big deal and, as a society, we value physical fitness. Fitness trackers are an 18 billion dollar industry because millions of people want to have access to tools for measuring their body's performance. The fitness tracker category was launched with simple pedometers but quickly expanded to making measurements of sleep, posture, balance, and diet. There is also a fitness data glut as our ability to track outruns our ability to understand, analyze, and use the numbers being generated. A couple of simple principles can help us get more out of these measurements.

Focus on metrics which:

- Relate directly to the goal.
- Are evidence-based.
- Are easy to gather.

Peter Drucker was fond of saying, "you can't manage what you can't measure." This is true as far as it goes but just gathering data is not enough. We need to also define success in a specific way and then track our progress toward, or away from, our goal. Consider this graph of Bob's journey to 10,000 steps.

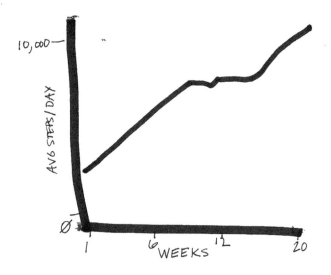

As you can see he started off full of enthusiasm and then reached a plateau. Three months in, Bob got discouraged and thought about quitting. Encouragement, education about plateaus, and a renewed focus on intermediate goals got him back on track. A wish is not a plan and a plan without measurements is merely a good intention. Without careful goal setting, proper preparation, access to the right equipment, and consistent measurement, and tracking, Bob's life would be very different today. All of this hard work might also help a talented young athlete take the state high jump title in May. Like Bob says, "It's all connected."

"Every traveler returns home."

--David Levithan

5

Home

Discover

Our culture's celebration of the single-family house as the ideal home often leads us to confuse a house with a home. Home is a place we make, not a place we find, and making a place to live into a home that is safe and secure is essential to the experience of well-being. People may spend money to travel to exotic places and enjoy new sights, sounds, and foods they find there but, sooner than they expect, they begin to pine for home. Every heart needs a home.

The idea of "home" means some-thing different to each of the billions of people living on this planet and there will never be a single objective standard for what it means to feel safe at home. Instead, we must search for the elements most commonly accepted as being important to feeling "at home." Chief among these is a desire to live in the place and manner of our own choosing. Indeed, it is the ability to obtain, and maintain, a place of one's own that most accurately marks the boundary separating adulthood from childhood. Being at home also means being able to (mostly!) do what you want, when you want. Mealtimes are set by people living in the house and, when we are at home, we can go to bed and rise in the morning at times that suit our own purposes, whatever they might be.

A sense of safety is closely associated with the feeling of being at home for most people. While safety might seem like an objective factor easily defined by numbers, that is not the case. In the context of LEADS, safety is defined by the people rather than regulations. We have volumes of reports documenting the risk of house fires, slips and falls in bathrooms, and carbon monoxide poisoning, but those numbers give only general guidance regarding what makes people feel safe. Millions of people have lived in institutions designed to reduce risk, and yet they never felt safe. Others have lived in fire trap shacks with leaking floors and felt as snug as bugs in rugs.

So, what's the best way to get to the bottom of people's experience with home and safety? The answer is simple: conversation.

Home Discovery Questions:

- Are you living where you want to live?

- Are you living how you want to live?

- What is the best thing about your home?

- What is the worst thing about your home?

- When do you feel most safe?

- When do you feel most unsafe?

- If you could describe your home in one word, what would it be?

Prioritize

Telling Alice's Story

"Get me out of here. I don't want to be here!"

Those were the first words Alice Trulove ever spoke to me. When I first met her, Alice was lying in a bed in a nursing home. It was a pretty good nursing home, according to the government's ranking system, but it was definitely not where she wanted to live. Before her fall, Alice was living at home with her garden and her cat. She was happy. If it wasn't for that rug, she would have stayed there. But the rug had other ideas. Alice was always an early riser and she was up before the sun that day. Her slipper caught the corner of a throw rug and she tripped and the fall broke her hip. She lay on the floor all day, which caused her to become dehydrated and confused. By the time the ambulance arrived, Alice was in very bad shape.

The hospital was not kind to Alice. She was exhausted but could not sleep because of the noises, and the nurses. Even though she was hungry, she was too tired to eat. Her hip replacement surgery was declared a success, but she got worse rather than better. Her wound became infected. Then came the pneumonia. In less than two weeks Alice went from puttering around her kitchen, and tending to her garden, to a shattered husk of a human being. Everyone said it was sad and everyone agreed, Alice couldn't go home again. Her daughter picked a nursing home on her side of town and Alice was placed in a semi-private room with a curtain separating her from a roommate she had never seen before.

Gradually, very gradually, Alice began to rebuild her strength. She put on a few pounds and learned to walk again. That's when I met her. She could hardly believe I was there to help her live the life she wanted to live. More than anything else, Alice wanted her life back -- and it was my job to help her make it happen.

Alice accepted the challenge of doing what needed to be done so she could be back at home, with her garden and her cat, before the snow flew.

Goal	Go Home
Specific	4
Measurable	3
Actionable	4
Realistic	2
Time-Bound	4
Total	15

The only thing I knew for certain was that the throw rug would have to go.

Empower

Resilience is the capacity to recover quickly from difficulties. Alice is a resilient person and always has been. She fought her way back from a broken hip, delirium induced by dehydration, sleep deprivation, acute undernutrition, a wound infection, pneumonia, and the loss of muscle mass, balance, and stamina. In the nursing home, she kept fighting. She got stronger, adapted to the challenges she faced and continued to see herself as a person who could live in her own home and be the boss of her own life. But even the most resilient and determined people can benefit from a helping hand.

Just recovering from her injury is not going to be enough for Alice; she will also need to be prepared and equipped for a new way of living in her own home. Therapists can help with the most basic tasks but there is more to life than sitting, walking, standing, and using a toilet. Being independent requires us to master a range of other skills called Instrumental Activities of Daily Living.

Instrumental Activities of Daily Living:

- **Managing finances**
- **Handling transportation**
- **Shopping**
- **Preparing meals**
- **Using the telephone or other communication devices**
- **Managing medications**
- **Doing laundry**
- **Housework**
- **Basic home maintenance**

Before the fall, Alice had ways of accomplishing all of these tasks. Now, she will need new ways of getting things done around the house. It will be important to make an inventory of the knowledge and tools she will need and make a plan that ensures she has what she needs to succeed.

Errors in her medical record will also need to be corrected. Alice's medical record now includes an inaccurate diagnosis of dementia. She did experience temporary confusion; she does not have dementia. Before the fall she was "sharp as a tack," as they say and she is just as sharp today. When she was admitted to the hospital the staff found her to be confused and anxious. This behavior was misinterpreted as dementia. It is important to remove inaccurate diagnoses because they lead to dangerous and ineffective treatments as well as unnecessary diagnostic testing.

Before the fall Alice took two pills a day and Tylenol as needed for aches and pains. Her medication list now totals 15 drugs, including two for dementia, which she does not have. This over-use of medications is called polypharmacy and it is the leading preventable cause of death among people over the age of 65. Engaging with a skilled primary care provider to trim the med list is crucial to long term success.

We can help Alice live at home using tools as simple as a reach extender and as complex as AI-enabled fall detection services. The precise tools depend on the circumstances and people's circumstances change all the time. We will also need to adapt Alice's house so it can once again be her home.

Ignite

Alice's New Story

Coming home was a dream come true for Alice. I stood by the door and watched as she walked from room to room and made sure everything was still there. Then she cried.

Alice is luckier than most. Too many people have their homes and all their possessions sold out from under them soon after they are placed in a nursing home. Her first night at home was blissfully uneventful and the newly accessible downstairs bathroom proved its worth. Now Alice and I face a new challenge -- helping her stay at home.To make this happen we will need to keep changing, keep adapting, keep up-to-date with who Alice is, and what she needs to live life on her own terms.

That will require us both to learn new things, master new skills, use new tools, and never lose sight of what matters most to Alice. It isn't that living at home is always best, or even the right thing to do; what matters most is what Alice wants and that's good enough for me.

The day may come when Alice is ready for a change, ready to close one chapter of her life and open another. When that day comes, I'll be ready.

We all have very different ideas about where and how we want to live. We also change our minds, as is our right. It is important to remember that sometimes (as in Alice's story) home is the best option but there are plenty of times when "staying at home" leads to social isolation, loneliness, hunger, depression, and loss of function. What's best for some can never be what's best for all. This is why it is

important to concentrate on autonomy, dignity, and choice rather than on
a house, a street, or a neighborhood.
Igniting and sustaining a passion for
and ability to live one's best life possible is what matters most.

Measure

Older people are more likely to be hospitalized than middle-aged people and, among older people, hospitalization rates increase shortly before admission to a long-term care facility.[19] While functional changes often precede hospitalization there are also well-documented declines in function after a hospital stay.[20] When we are helping people assess the attainability of a goal (such as returning home) it is important to carefully assess a person's function.

According to current research, these areas stand out as being especially relevant to a person's ability to function independently:[21]
- Gait and Balance
- Hearing Acuity
- Visual Acuity
- Urinary Continence

- Nutritional Status
- List of Medications

When it comes to determining where we live and how we live, function interacts with place. If Alice's home was a treehouse with a rope ladder it is unlikely she would have been able to return home. There needs to be a fit between a person and the place they call home. Just as people can build fitness, places can be made more fit for older occupants. Once again, measurement is our friend.

A walkthrough of a home can identify simple changes that can make a big difference.

Kitchen

- No stove shut off
- Shiny/Slippery floor

Kitchen Con't.

- Multi-tasking
- Inaccessible high cabinets
- Low chair height
- Spoiled food in refrigerator

Bathroom

- Low toilet height
- Shiny/Slippery floor
- Bath mat trip hazard
- No tub grab bars/ No bath bench
- Dim lighting
- Humidity leading to spoilage of meds

Bedroom

- Low bed height
- Throw rugs
- Dim lighting

- Low chair height
- No night light

Walkways

- Stairs
- Throw rugs
- Dim lighting
- Thresholds
- Obstacles in the pathway

Once we have a good understanding of the person (and his/her function) and the place he/she wants to call home, we can go to work optimizing the fit between the person and the environment.

With money you can buy...
    a house, but not a home.
    a clock, but not time.
    a bed, but not sleep.
    a book, but not knowledge.
    a doctor, but not good health.
    a position, but not respect.
    blood, but not life.

        -- Anonymous

6
Money

Discover

During the Great Depression, a well-known writer was having drinks with a rising star on Broadway. He told her about the movie offers he was getting and she responded, "Listen and take my advice. Don't overlook the money part of it. I've been poor and I've been rich. Rich is better!" Rich may be better than poor but the relationship between money and well-being is, well, it's complicated.

Money can't buy us love, or happiness, but it is exceptionally useful for obtaining food, clothing, shelter, and medicine and those things are hard to do without. Indeed, being very poor is associated with both a shorter lifespan and reduced life satisfaction. Nearly 50 years ago, economist Richard Easterlin took an in-depth look at the relationship between money and happiness and discovered that, when you look at people who are living above the poverty line, it is relative income, rather than absolute income, that tracks most closely with happiness. When it comes to cash, keeping up with the Joneses is what matters most.

The very rich do encounter problems related to their wealth. For example, pop psychology offers us the concept of "affluenza" which is said to be a malaise affecting wealthy people, symptoms of which include a lack of motivation, feelings of guilt, and a sense of isolation. While some wealthy people do have problems with money, the most significant financial issues relate to people who are of limited means. Nearly all of these folks have access to food, housing, and medicine but the ice they are skating on is very thin indeed. The data on food insecurity among older Americans tells the tale.

- Of the ten states with the highest rates of senior food insecurity, nine are in the south.
- Almost one-third of food insecure seniors are disabled.
- Nearly 65 percent of food-insecure seniors are younger than age 69.
- Nearly one in every five seniors living with grandchildren is food insecure.
- African American or Hispanic are disproportionately impacted: 17 percent of African American seniors and 18 percent of Hispanic seniors are food insecure, compared to 7 percent of Cauca-

sian seniors.

According to the American Psychological Association, three-quarters of the people surveyed said they had stressed about money at some point in the last month, while more than a quarter said they are stressed about money most or all of the time.[22]

Money Discovery Questions:

- **Do you worry about your finances?**

- **Do other people worry about your finances?**

- **Are your finances getting better, getting worse, or staying about the same?**

- **Does paying the bills cause stress?**

Prioritize

Irene's Story

I grew up poor but it never bothered me much because every-body I knew back then was poor. My dad worked at the mill and my mom looked after us kids and took in washing. She would iron clothes while the rest of us watched the television after dinner. All three of my brothers went to work at the mill with my dad but I had a head for numbers like they used to say. Mom decided I should go to college and become an accountant. Going to school seemed a lot better than taking in washing to me so I did what she said. It wasn't easy but I graduated and became a CPA. I never got married, well, I guess I was married to my work and I spent 40 years looking after other people's money. Now, I'm retired.

I guess it's because I didn't have a family of my own that I looked after everybody else the way I did. I put two nieces and four nephews through college. I've paid for, I don't know how many, cars, and apartments and house down payments. I paid for mom's nursing home before she died. I'm glad I could do all that. My family's not poor anymore.

I kept enough for myself but I'm not rich. I've seen rich, and I never wanted that life. But, you know, I've been retired for 15 years now and I realize how people move on. I don't hear from my nieces and nephews the way I used to. You can't blame them, they're busy with their own families. But I do get to thinking... It's really just me now. I'm on my own. How much longer do I have? Will the money run out? If I make it to 90, who would take care of me? I just don't know. So here I am with more money than I ever expected to have-- and I still worry. To be honest, it keeps me up at night.

> ## Potential Goals:
>
> A: Cut expenses by 10 percent.
>
> B: Download Quickbooks.
>
> C: Set up an appointment with a certified retirement financial advisor in the next month.
>
> D: Find a part-time job to boost income.

Goal List	A	B	C	D
Specific	3	5	5	3
Measurable	2	2	3	4
Actionable	5	3	4	2
Realistic	1	3	4	2
Time-Bound	4	1	5	3
Total	15	14	21	14

Irene accepted the challenge of setting up an appointment with a certified retirement financial advisor within the next month.

Empower

Irene's story is centered around financial anxiety rather than financial need. Her anxiety is due to two factors. First, as she has grown older, her once close connections to extended family members have weakened. She feels, as many older people do, that she does not want to burden them with her worries. Also, her self image is one of a benefactor who enables others to reach for their dreams. She now realizes, perhaps correctly, that those she sacrificed for may not be willing to sacrifice for her. True or not, this idea leads to her focus ever more on her dwindling financial resources and this leads to financial anxiety.

It might seem there is little could be done for a certified public accountant with forty years of experi- ence-- but that would be wrong.

1. We can encourage Irene to stop and breathe. Anxiety creates a self-stoking cycle that disconnects from the actual facts on the ground. Unfortunately, accountants rarely receive training in stress reduction. Struggling

with a practical problem in the context of significant anxiety can actually make matters worse. Reducing anxiety helps people more accurately assess their options and act accord- ingly.

2. This is a good time to encour- age mindfulness. Irene can learn specific skills she can use to calm her mind. She has much to be proud of and her accomplishments need to be celebrated. It can also be especially useful to ask her to think about what she would say to a friend who was worried about money. Given her personality, it is likely she would show that friend every kindness. She can do the same for herself.

3. Financial anxiety is often due

to a combination of internal and external issues. Internal issues are related to our own thoughts and actions. External issues are related to the economy as a whole, such as a drop in the stock market. It is important to face the future head-on and place the focus on actions you can take that will make a difference. The act of making the implicit (I am worried about running out of money.) explicit (I am going to take steps to secure my future.) can, by itself, relieve a great deal of anxiety.

On a practical level, we can help Irene select a Certified Trust and Financial Advisor (CTFA) and arrange a consultation. To earn this certification a financial professional must have work experience, pass a comprehensive exam, and agree to abide by a strict code of ethics. This certification is offered by the American Bankers Association and is available to trust and wealth management professions that offer fee-based services.

The consultation can help Irene make a plan and when she has a plan we can help her carry it out by equipping her with tools and experiences that help her track her progress, and connect her to social experiences aligned with her self image as a person who helps others. AARP runs a large national tax preparation program that helps hundreds of thousands of people every year and it relies entirely on volunteers -- people like Irene.

Ignite

Irene's New Story

I see my new financial advisor every six months and we run through all the numbers. It feels so good. "Plan the work and work the plan." That's what he always says, and he's right.

Something happened over the holidays I never, in my life, thought would happen. Ricky's the youngest of my oldest brother's boys; he's a good boy but I never hear from him. When he called me out of the blue I knew right away something was up. He said he was out of work and behind on his rent. He asked me for two thousand dollars. Like I say, he's a good boy but I told him I'd get back to him. I called George, he's my advisor, I called him right up and told him about it. We agreed it wasn't in the plan. So, for the first time ever. I said no.

I said no to Ricky!

Now I won't deny I might have gotten him a really nice Christmas present but I didn't go over my budget for the holidays so no harm done. In March, Ricky called again and said he had a new job and things were looking up. I am so proud of that young man.

Like I said before, Ricky is going to be fine-- and so am I.

Helping Irene stay on track with her financial advisor and the plan they developed together is easier because we also acknowledged how anxiety can cloud judgment and paralyze decision-making. The work we do together on mindfulness has helped her in other ways as well. She finds she worries

less overall and has a greater appre-
ciation for the many blessings (as she
calls them) in her life.

Measure

Arthur Somers Roche wrote, "Anxiety is a thin stream of fear trickling through the mind. If encouraged, it cuts a channel into which all other thoughts are drained." It might be money. It might be love. It might be loss. The things we worry about vary widely. The impact, however, is universal. Worry and anxiety diminish our capacity for action. That's important because the antidote to anxiety is action. Fortunately, there are tools for measuring anxiety and those tools can guide us toward a happier, less stressful life.[23]

The Geriatric Anxiety Scale:

Below is a list of common symptoms of anxiety or stress. Please read each item in the list carefully. Indicate how often you have experienced each symptom during the past week, including today.

* Not at all (0), Sometimes (1), Most of the time (2), All of the time (3)

    1. I was irritable.
    2. I felt detached or isolated from others.
    3. I felt like I was in a daze.
    4. I had a hard time sitting still.
    5. I could not control my worry.
    6. I felt restless, keyed up, or on edge.
    7. I felt tired.
    8. My muscles were tense.
    9. I felt like I had no control over my life.

10. I felt like something terrible was going to happen to me.

The raw score can be assessed using this table:

Raw Score	Anxiety Category
1-6	Minimal
7-9	Mild
10-11	Moderate
12+	Severe

Irene agreed to take this quiz every three months. These were her scores over the past year.

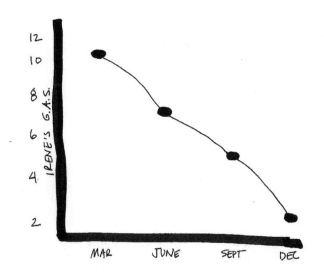

Living with more confidence and less worry opens the door to possibilities yet to be explored.

What a piece of work is a man!
How noble in reason, how infinite
in faculty! In form and moving
how express and admirable!

--- William Shakespeare

7
Thinking

Discover

Nearly four centuries ago the French philosopher Descartes confronted a difficult question: "How can I know for certain I exist?" The answer he came up with (cogito, ergo sum) ultimately formed the basis of Western philosophy. Translated into English this means, "I think, therefore I am." Descartes explained his reasoning something like this...

If you can doubt, you can think.
If you can think you must exist.
I doubt.
Therefore
I think
Therefore

I exist.

Pretty cool.

People understand that thinking is central to our existence and they fear dementia because they see the loss of memory as a threat to their existence. People lie awake at night, staring into the dark, and wonder -- "If my memory goes -- will I exist?" A National Institute on Aging study, which has tracked a thousand men and women since 1958 to observe changes that come with age, found concerns about declining sexual interest and personality changes, among other things -- but memory loss is what people talk about most.

Currently, there is no known cure for any of the most common types of dementia and the lack of effective treatments fosters both fear and ignorance. People mix together terms like

Alzheimer's, frontotemporal, and Lewy Body without understanding that these are specific forms of the general condition we call "dementia." Dementia is a common condition but few people can offer a precise definition for it.

Dementia is the gradual, irreversible loss of previously attained cognitive function.

Although dementia develops gradually, it can be revealed quickly. Many have commented on how the death of a spouse suddenly reveals how heavily the widow or widower had been depending on his or her partner.

Although people can have good days and bad days, dementia never gets better. A person's cognition may vary significantly but the overall trend is toward greater impairment.

One test of cognitive impairment is to ask a person to count backward from 100 by sevens. (100, 93, 86, 79...) Someone who can not do this but was never good at mental arithmetic may not have dementia. A math professor who can pass this test may actually be living with dementia. Dementia has to be understood as a change from a person's baseline abilities.

Just asking older people about their memory can provoke anxiety. The writer Samuel Johnson long ago remarked, "There is a wicked inclination in most people to suppose an old man decayed in his intellect. If a young or middle-aged man . . . does not recollect where he laid his hat, it is nothing. But if the same inattention is discovered in an old man, people will shrug their shoulders and say, 'His memory is going.'" It's OK to ask questions like those below.

Thinking Discovery Questions:

- **Do you worry about your memory?**

- **Do other people worry about your memory?**

Prioritize

Carol's Story

It started with little things. He'd go upstairs and then come back and laugh about forgetting why he went up there. Then he started forgetting things we'd talked about. Nothing important, just little things, but after a while, the little things got bigger. Floyd always paid the bills. The first of the every month he'd sit down and write checks and tally everything up in a little book he kept. He started joking that after 50 years of marriage it was

my turn to pay the bills. That's when
I should have known but we just kept
going, living the way we always lived.

The walls caved in the day the
police called. Floyd had taken the dog
out for a walk and gotten lost. They
picked him up on the other side of
town and brought him home. I called
the doctor right away. She said to
bring him in next week for a check-up.
Next week! My world was falling apart
but she said it wasn't an emergency.
Floyd denied everything. He blamed
it on the heat and said he'd just made
one wrong turn and said it was no big
deal. But it was a big deal. That was
the longest week of my life.

We saw the doctor; she asked
a lot of questions and ordered a lot
of tests. I guess the good news was
he didn't have a brain tumor but the
bad news just about killed me. She
said Floyd had Alzheimer's and had

probably had it for years, it's just that we were starting to notice it. I was sick to my stomach. All those times I wondered if something was wrong, I was right, there really was something wrong.

Floyd took it so much better than me. He said it was no big deal, he felt great and said I shouldn't worry so much. Doctors make mistakes, he said. But the doctor was right. She put him on some pills, Floyd never had to take medicine before. But, other than that, not much changed for him.

For me, it was like the world had ended. I couldn't let him out of my sight. I couldn't sleep because I worried he would wander off. I took on paying the bills, and fixing things around the house. Floyd just drifted away from me. He'd sit in his recliner for hours, he'd eat, he'd smile when I talked to him but I felt like my best friend had left me. So that's where I am. I'm still married but I've never felt more alone, or more afraid.

There is an unfortunate tendency to believe that a diagnosis of dementia impacts only the person receiving the diagnosis. In fact, the diagnosis can have a larger initial impact on members of the family. It has been observed that, over time, family members tend to "outsource" certain cognitive functions to other members of the family. For example, Floyd "did the bills" for half a century. As Floyd's cognition changed, and he stopped doing some of "his jobs," it was Carol who felt the impact most keenly. She was also coping with cognitive change but for very different reasons.

Potential Goals:

A: Facilitate a conversation between Floyd and Carol that explores their future together.

B: Help Carol support Floyd's continued independence in new ways.

C: Arrange respite care so Carol can join and participate in a weekly support group.

D: Educate Carol on the importance of helping Floyd continue to find meaning and happiness in his life.

Goal List	A	B	C	D
Specific	3	1	4	3
Measurable	2	2	3	3
Actionable	5	3	4	3
Realistic	3	3	4	3
Time-Bound	1	1	5	2
Total	14	10	20	14

Carol accepted the challenge of receiving respite care so she could participate in a weekly spouses support group.

Empower

Fear and ignorance are powerful allies. Many people fear dementia more than death and that fear often prevents them from learning more about this condition. Carol feels guilty she didn't "do something" sooner but, in reality, there is nothing she could have done. Now that the diagnosis has been made, her constant worry hampers her ability to connect with and enjoy the company of a man who is, by clinical measures, very early in the progression.

There is great truth in the idea that education is the antidote to both ignorance and fear and accurate information about dementia can empower Carol to change her own thoughts and actions. She has the power to change how she copes with these changes and, in doing so, significantly improve her quality of life. This is a brand new situation for her. She has never been married to a person living with dementia before and it is going to take time, and access to new knowledge and tools, to find a new normal.

One social practice that has proven its worth to people in Carol's situation is the peer support group. Life is strange, and difficult, and it really helps to sit down with people who know in their bones what you are feeling and what you are going through.[24] The Alzheimer's Association convenes groups for caregivers, individuals living with Alzheimer's, and others coping with the disease. Some are led by peers, some by professionals. Depending on where you live, there may be specialized groups for children, individuals with younger-onset and early-stage Alzheimer's, and adult caregivers. In Carol's case, her participation is contingent on respite services that allow her to feel at ease while she is participating in the group.

Ignite

Carol's New Story

What a difference a year makes. Floyd is doing so much better than I ever expected and, in a strange way, we are closer than we've ever been. So many things have changed but so many things are the same. Our daughter Debbie took over the job of paying the bills so that's been a huge load off my mind. The Tuesday group has helped me so much, I just don't feel overwhelmed anymore. Yesterday, the group leader asked me if I would consider taking the group facilitator training. He said I'd be great at leading my own group! Just the thought of it scares me but, after what we've been through, I'm pretty sure I could do it. I'll talk it over with Floyd. He's different than he used to be but he's still Floyd and I married him because he had a good head on his shoulders.

The house has some gadgets that help Floyd be safe and help me worry less. I don't really know how it all works but if I press this button they say help will come. I know this is just for now. We'll need more help when the time comes. There is no cure for Alzheimer's and we need to live every day like it's our last. Turns out, that's not such a bad way to go through life. Every day is a gift-- that's why they call it the present!

Because dementia unfolds grad-ually, there can never be a single set of knowledge and tools suited to every situation. People change and people living with dementia change in ways that can be hard for family members to understand. **We live in a world**

designed for, built for, and run for the benefit of people who do not have dementia. This means that, as people move through the experience of living with dementia, they find themselves in a world less and less suited to their needs. This gradual disconnection is distressing for everyone involved. But it can be different.

We can use a deeper understanding of dementia and the changes it brings to people's lives to create a process of continuous adaptation. New circumstances require new tools and new knowledge. This is true at every point in the process, not just at the beginning -- or the end.

Measure

There are many tools and scales designed to measure the cognitive abilities of people living with dementia. They all provide useful measurements that, when used over time, provide valuable information about the nature of the cognitive change. But the impact of dementia is felt by the whole family, not just the person receiving the diagnosis. In particular, the people most involved with caregiving also have their lives forever altered. Researchers have found caregivers experience a 63 percent increase in the risk of death over 4 years compared to non-caregivers.[25]

The stress of caregiving is real and is deserving of much more attention than it receives. The Kingston Caregiver Stress Scale is especially helpful in this regard because, instead of asking one question, "How much stress do you feel?", it probes beneath the surface with a set of ten questions related to potential sources of caregiver stress. It is also easy to use:[26]

Caregiver Stress Scale

Some people report feelings of stress surrounding certain aspects of caregiving. To what extent, if any, do these apply to you in your role of caregiving to your spouse or relative?

Using a 5 point rating scale, where 1 equals no stress and 5 equals extreme stress, rate the stress or frustration you feel surrounding the following issues.

1. Are you having feelings of being overwhelmed, over-worked, and/or overburdened?
2. Has there been a change in your relationship with your spouse/relative?
3. Have you noticed any changes in your social life?
4. Are you having any conflicts with your previous daily com-mitments (work/volunteering)?

5. Do you have feelings of being confined or trapped by the responsibilities or demands of caregiving?

6. Do you ever have feelings related to a lack of confidence in your ability to provide care?

7. Do you have concerns regarding the future care needs of your spouse/relative?

8. Are you having any conflicts within your family over care decisions?

9. Are you having any conflicts within your family over the amount of support you are receiving in providing care?

10. Are you having any financial difficulties associated with caregiving?

Over the course of a year, periodic measurements showed that, even as Floyd's condition changed, Carol was able to adapt to those changes with decreasing levels of stress and worry.

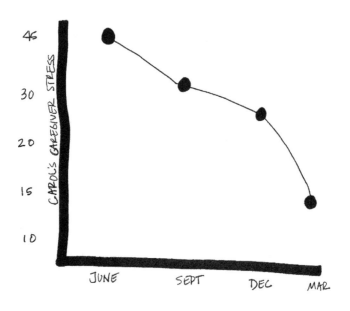

Who are you? (Who are you?
Who, who, who, who?)

-- Pete Townsend

8
Being

Discover

Our identity is actually an evolving intersection between our genes, our culture, and the people we love and care for, as well as those we have harmed, or who have harmed us. These connections inform who we were, who we are, and who we may still become.[27] While there isn't much we can do about our genes, or the culture we inhabit, the people who are closest to us play a large and often unrecognized role (for good and ill) in how we see ourselves. A "long life" is made up of a succession of distinct identities joined end to end and, if we are lucky, this whole becomes greater than the sum of its parts.

Research reveals positive associations between identity, well-being, and a willingness to do for others.[28] A Swedish study explored this terrain using data generated from in-depth interviews with 884 people. The results highlight a complex interaction between:

(1) personal identity and personal well-being;
(2) collective identity and collective well-being; and
(3) collective identity and a collective willingness to sacrifice.

We all know the phrase, "It takes a village to raise a child." What we too often fail to understand is that "it takes a village for you -- to be you." Our personal and collective identities overlap and actively reinforce each other. This is a valuable insight because as we get older, our network of social connections can begin to fray.

Much has been written about social isolation and the burden of loneliness but what has yet to be fully recognized is the degree to which having a sense of identity (me-ness) depends on social connections strong enough for us to be willing to sacrifice for them (we-ness). Our "me" needs a "we" in order to thrive. Knowing this can help us help older people experience a more powerful sense of identity and with it a stronger grasp on health and well-being.

Being Discovery Questions:

- **What do you do for others?**

- **What do you do for yourself?**

- **What do you do for society?**

Prioritize

Floyd's Story

Carol took this whole thing a lot harder than I did. I just thought 'that's life;' sometimes you get the lemons and sometimes... Anyway, my dad, Floyd Merrick Sr., had Alzheimer's so I know how it goes. It's just that one day I got a little confused, then I'm at the doctor. All of a sudden Carol is a mother hen. She never let me out of her sight.

I tried to tell her it was going to be all right but she wouldn't listen. So I was stuck at home. The only thing she'd let me do is sit in my chair and watch TV, and I hate TV. The medicine they gave me made my stomach hurt and I didn't want to take it but Carol started crying when I said that so I took the pills. The damn stuff didn't do me any good.

Look, I might be an old guy
and I might be losing my marbles
but it's not like my life is over. I like
getting up early. I like my coffee. I like
walking the dog. I like lots of stuff but
after the doctor told me what I had,
Carol and Debbie treated me like I was
already dead.

I say back off! Let me live my
life! I'm the same person I always was
but now, I have some trouble remem-
bering things! Things could be a whole
lot worse and they could be a whole
lot better if people would treat me
like I'm Floyd Merrick, Jr. and not like
I'm some kind of basket case. There's
plenty of things I can do.

A diagnosis of dementia brings
profound changes into people's lives

and, as of this writing, there is no cure for this condition. Our well meaning society, neighbors, family, and friends unfortunately add to the burden by limiting and restricting people living with dementia long before there is a practical reason to do so. Old friends drift away, believing they have nothing to say to someone with a diagnosis of dementia. Family relationships degenerate into struggles over safety and control -- and the love gets lost. **Our identity isn't just a function of our brain power; it also includes how people see us and how we are reflected in their eyes when they look into ours.**

Floyd needs help holding onto his identity as he goes on the dementia journey. That means supporting his sense of self-worth, autonomy and dignity and helping the people around him see him as he wishes to be seen. Floyd is a husband, a father, a friend and a person "with a good head on his shoulders." None of those things have changed.

Potential Goals:

A: Arrange for Floyd to meet weekly with a "dementia coach."

B: Get connected to inspiring videos showing how other people are living with dementia.

C: Arrange a follow-up appointment to address medication side-effects.

D: Arrange for a care aide to accompany Floyd on his walks.

Goal List	A	B	C	D
Specific	4	4	4	3
Measurable	3	1	1	1
Actionable	5	3	4	3
Realistic	3	3	4	2
Time-Bound	4	1	3	3
Total	19	14	16	12

Floyd accepts the challenge of meeting with a dementia coach for an hour each week for the next year.

Empower

When we are young we work hard to figure out who we are and what we want out of life. This is sometimes called "finding yourself." This is a good thing, and everyone from our teachers, to our families, to our friends try to help us along the way.

In mid-life most people experience the pressure that comes with having multiple important identities all with overlapping demands. Mother - check. Sister - check. Wife - check. Wage earner - check. Friend - check. As we get older, this crush subsides and people can once again face the question: "Who am I?"

Illnesses -- like dementia -- and new roles -- like widowhood -- make this question even more challenging to answer. What matters most is understanding that in the book of life, like in any good book, the most interesting chapters come near the end. We can find a new identity but, just as when we were young, it helps to be prepared and equipped for the journey ahead.

Dementia Journey Essential Prep:

The idea that aging equals decline is almost never challenged. Ageist prejudice limits the scope of possibilities and damages older people's inherent capacity for growth. When we recognize the value of every age we are much better prepared to grow into a new role and spend less time brooding about losing our grip on an old role.

- Research on happiness suggests that, statistically speaking, the happiest decade of life is the seventies. To be sure, some people are very unhappy in their seventies but, overall, the arrow of happiness points upward from the late forties on.
- Any parent can tell you that certain elements of a child's personality are baked in the cake and there is little that

can be done to change them. This is also true for older people. The difference is a lifetime of experience. Living a long life as an introvert, for example, helps older people get closer to being the person they were always meant to be. **Approached skillfully, aging doesn't defeat us, it completes us.**

- Living in an older body also makes enabling technology more important than ever. We can use the most advanced technology to relieve pain, enhance vision and hearing, and fill the gaps as our short term memory changes with age. There has never, in the history of the world, been a better time to be an older person.

Floyd Merrick, Jr. is a person. He

is living his own, never to be dupli-
cated, life. We can help him enjoy his
journey to the fullest by offering him
access to the knowledge and tools he
needs, and nothing more.

Ignite

Floyd's New Story

Carol has been great. She laughs
so much more. I think the group helps
her. I don't like things like participating in support groups. My coach says
I'm the real Alzheimer's expert around
here. Carol doesn't have it. I do. I
tell Carol when she does things that
bother me. Like when she hid all the
kitchen knives. That was crazy! We
walk the dog together now. I like that.

I decided to stop taking that terrible medicine and I feel a lot better.
People say I should take it but it didn't

work for me. I talk to Alexa and tell her to remind me of things I need to do. She never forgets! I forget. She doesn't. Alexa tells jokes too.

Some people say you forget who you are but I haven't forgotten who I am. I'm Floyd Merrick, Jr.. I forget other people's names but it doesn't bother me. I just laugh. If I laugh they laugh. Laughing makes everything easier.

I don't know how much time I have left. Nobody does! It doesn't really matter because we all die. What can I say, I'm me and I'm going to keep being me, until the end comes.

Floyd is living with a terminal condition called Alzheimer's Disease. He knows he is going to die and we can honor his insight by acknowledging this painful truth. Now is the perfect time to talk with him about how he would like his life to end and to establish written guidelines governing his passing.

Measure

Shadows and doubt are a small price to pay for living in a world of light and possibility. We are all mortal beings and a thoughtful exploration of one's own death is, perhaps, the highest expression of identity. There is nothing more personal, or intimate, than the act of leaving this world. Too often, the treatments people choose to accept, or refuse, near the end of their lives are very different from the treatments they actually receive. This gap is primarily due to the fact that only about a third of Americans complete any form of advance planning document.[29] At the most basic level these documents include:

- A living will -- a living will is only used at the end of life if a person is terminally ill or permanently unconscious. It describes the medical treatments a person would want or not want to receive near the end of life.
- A durable power of attorney for health care is a legal document which names a person to be a proxy (agent) to make all health care decisions if a person becomes unable to do so.
- A do not resuscitate (DNR) order governs the use of machines and methods used to re-start someone's heart and breathing using methods such as CPR (cardiopulmonary resuscitation) and AED (automated external defibrillator).

- An organ and tissue donation codifies wishes regarding the use of body parts after death.
- It is likely that when the end of Floyd's life draws near, he will lack the decision making capacity needed to wrestle with these questions so the time to explore them is now. This is also a good time to help Carol and Debbie complete these documents for themselves. The measure of success?

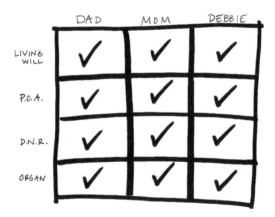

Floyd, Carol, and their daughter Debbie have each completed the end of life documents described above.

"The purpose of life
is a life of purpose."

-- Richard Leider

9
Purpose

Discover

Small things make a big difference. A wink, a smile, a single kind word can alter the complexion of our day. While there may seem to be little difference between what we "have to do" and what we "want to do" appreciating this distinction can change our lives. Moving deliberately from a life of "have to do" to a life of "want to do" is the first step on the road to living one's life with purpose. Everyone spends time on their "have to dos." The question is, how much time are we investing in our "want to dos?" As we grow older we can change our priorities, and our way of living. Aging enables living with purpose, and living with purpose is fun.

Does purpose matter? A JAMA study published in 2019 showed that, among people over the age of 50, having a strong life purpose leads to improvements in both physical and mental health and enhances overall quality of life.[30] A survey of US Military veterans revealed that a strong connection to purpose was associated with greater resilience and correlated positively with recovery from PTSD.[31]

Richard Leider has written about a process of "unpacking and repacking" that can accelerate a person's journey into living with greater purpose and meaning. We pack our lives with the things we need to succeed in the tumult of adulthood, raising a family, pursuing a career, and paying the bills. These things are essential to the middle part of life and sometimes people hold fast to them for so long they become burdens rather than pleasures.

Our friends, family, and society do us no favors when it comes to unpacking and repacking because they so often celebrate the lack of change in older people's lives as evidence of success. Younger people often use the word "still" when they are talking about older people they admire. "My grandmother is 86 and she *still* drives!" That word, still, serves to remind older people that as long as they can live like a younger person they will still have a place in society. **The act of holding fast to habits and routines that no longer serve us well diminishes our potential for growth.** Unpack! Repack! Let go! Take hold! Have fun! Life is best when we direct our energy toward what we want to do and be.

| Purpose Discovery Questions: |

- **What matters most to you?**

- **When was the last time you laughed out loud?**

- **Can you tell me about the last time you had fun?**

- **Whose life did you make better in the last week?**

Prioritize

Tom's Story

I was drafted into the Army straight out of high school in '69. Boot camp was the opposite of the summer of love I can tell you that. After boot camp they sent me to Advanced Infantry Training school; that was at Fort Dix too. Vietnam was at the height of the fighting. The war had the country wrapped around the axle. My dad was in the Army in World War II and he went off to fight so I did too. It's not like I had anything better to do. People like us don't go to college.

A land mine tore up my arm and killed two of my buddies on August 8, 1970. I was choppered out. The docs couldn't save it and they amputated about midway between the elbow and shoulder. There wasn't much else they could do. Hell, I couldn't even use a hook. People stare so I just tell them I left my right arm in Vietnam.

Came home and wound up being the best damned one armed forklift operator you ever saw. Worked in the same warehouse for 35 years but for five different companies. I used to tell the new bosses "I come with the ware-house." Got married. Drank too much. Got divorced. Got married again.

Stopped drinking and had it good till she got cancer. My sweet Linda fought like hell but the cancer got into her bones. Never had kids. Been retired a while. Now it's just me and god damned TV.

Fifty years gone by since I shipped out from Dix and American boys are still out there still getting their arms and legs blown off. Some things never change. I've got diabetes and high blood pressure. The doc says if I don't do something he's gonna have to cut my right foot off. He doesn't scare me. The doc can say whatever he wants but I'll tell you what, somebody should do something for those boys.

Potential Goals:

A: Arrange a consultation with a dietician to improve compliance with diet and medication.

B: Arrange second opinion with vascular surgeon regarding need for amputation.

C: Challenge himself to "do something for those boys" now, before it's too late.

D: Encourage regular exercise.

Goal List	A	B	C	D
Specific	3	5	4	3
Measurable	2	2	3	5
Actionable	5	3	4	1
Realistic	1	3	4	2
Time-Bound	4	1	5	3
Total	15	14	20	14

Tom accepts the challenge to "do something for those boys" now, before it's too late.

Empower

Tom's Purpose

I turned off the TV and turned on the radio because the radio doesn't rile me up the way the TV does. The first time I heard about Ernie Andrus was on a morning news show. That son of a bitch was a medic in World War II and there he was, 93 years old, walking all the way across the country to raise money to honor the men who died at Normandy. It took him 2 years, 10 months and 13 days to get the job done but he did it, California to Georgia, Pacific to Atlantic. That got me to thinking. Ernie served with my dad. But there he was -- doing something. I figured if Ernie could do it, so could I.

Purpose is like the heart of a star, it radiates passion and passion can change the world. When Tom found his new purpose, his eyes lit up. He also found that "doing something for those boys" requires much more than just good intentions.

Turning intention into action calls for two very different types of growth and development.

A diabetic, hypertensive, self-proclaimed "king of the recliner" needs to learn about MESH (Move, Eat, Sleep, Heal) and start preparing for a 3,000 mile expedition. He will need to understand his body, and his chronic conditions much better than he does today. This will take time, and effort.

Move -- a one-armed sedentary man in his seventies can't just start walking across America. Getting ready is going to require work on balance, posture, and stamina. He'll also need the right footwear because a blister could lead to serious complications.

Eat -- Before he decided to follow Ernie's lead, Tom's diet consisted mainly of boxed macaroni and cheese, toast, and raspberry jam, and some-times the jam went on the macaroni and cheese. Now, he needs to learn to eat right. Also, he'd been managing his diabetes on autopilot but changes in diet and exercise mean he'll have to learn how to adjust his dosages to fit his intake and exercise levels.

Sleep -- Before he started, Tom complained bitterly about his lack of sleep. He needed coaching on proper sleep hygiene and he very reluctantly moved the TV out of the bedroom. A better diet, increasing physical activity and discontinuing a couple of medica-tions that had been interfering with his sleep also helped.

Heal -- Amputees understand there is no going back to the way things used to be and most work hard to create a new normal. As the world's best one-armed forklift operator, Tom understood the need to move forward. But losing one's sense of purpose represents a very different, invisible, kind of amputation. When Tom left work he was finally free from having a boss, but he also suffered a blow to his identity. Now, he is growing into a new purpose with a new passion that is demanding everything he has to give.

Truly helping others requires sacrifice. Tom's new willingness to sacrifice his time and effort on behalf of others will require him to break out of his shell and build new social networks that can help him share his purpose and passion. He'll have to do this work in person and online and those are not skills he has honed in the past. A computer with an internet connection will be essential to finding the people who will pledge donations. Finally, Tom needs to master the management of his diabetes, embrace new communication devices, and build the circle of supporters who can help him turn his passion into progress.

Ignite

Tom's New Story

It was a hell of a fight, mostly between me and the recliner. But I won. I'm doing something for the boys. People say to me you're too old! You're never going to make it! I tell them I'm just following in Ernie's footsteps. From San Diego to Georgia's St. Simon's Island, every mile I walk I'm making money for Operation Second Chance.

I'll admit I was kind of a mess when I started all this. Mainly because

I didn't want anybody to tell me what to do. That's the nice thing about being retired; it's the first time in my life I didn't have a boss. Might sound weird but the job kept me between the guardrails. I worked hard and I'll be damned if I didn't look forward to the weekend. After I left, the days just kind of blended together. Hell, the years blended together. When they challenged me to stop whining and actually do something, it made me mad. But they were right; actions speak louder than words.

Tom's new purpose carried him, and many others, very far indeed. After his first walk across America raised $51,439 he decided to start a non-profit. A couple of years later he made his second walk across America, this time accompanied by veterans of Iraq and Afghanistan. He stopped needing medication for his high blood pressure and his diabetes and there was no more talk about amputations. It turns out that San Diego was nicer than he ever thought it would be and he moved there so he could enjoy the weather, and be close to the veterans being cared for at the VA hospital.

He met his new best friend, Susie Brown, a Navy Veteran who lost a limb to an IED in 2003. She always reminds Tom it's not just "the boys" who can use a helping hand.

Measure

We know the power of passion when we feel it and we know it can change lives but measuring passion and purpose is a very tricky business. We see passion and purpose mainly in the changes they bring into our lives, and the lives of others.

For Tom:

- Weight: Decreased his body mass index (BMI) by losing fat and building muscle. His BMI dropped from 34.5 to 26.1.
- Blood Glucose: His HbA1c, a measure of overall blood sugar control, declined from 7.2 percent to 4.3 percent. He no longer requires medication but he does watch his diet carefully.
- Miles: Tom has walked across America three times. The first time he went alone; the other two journeys were made alongside fellow veterans.

For Others:

- Tom has raised $287,932 for the purchase of prosthetic limbs.
- He has done 512 press interviews.
- He has posed for 10,620 selfies as he walked. Those pictures have been shared millions of times on the web and have raised awareness of issues related to disabled veterans nationwide.

The ripple effects of Tom's purpose and passion are incalculable.

10
Using Your Life Plan

"It's about you." --Joel Theisen

Discover

From our first day to our last we are connected to others. Our family teaches us how to live and how to love. For a small number of us, those lessons are all we need to thrive. Most of us, however, also need our friends, our teachers, and our mentors to help us find our way. It's about finding our way forward. Making a plan for our life is just another step forward on this journey. The process always begins with a conversation with someone we trust. Conversation leads us to the less visited corners of our lifelong hopes and dreams.

The lives we live are journeys of discovery. **We make plans because we sense a gap between the way things are and the way we want them to be.** Something's not right and we feel a need to fix it. But what exactly is it that needs fixing? Only you know. Only you can decide where the next chapter of your life will take you, and how you will get there.

Prioritize

It's been said that "to live is to choose" But, choosing is difficult. Everytime we say "yes" to one possibility we must say "no" to another. When we are traveling in a car we choose the route to our destination but we have access to electronic maps, street signs, and friendly locals who can assure us, "it's straight through three lights and then take the left." As we get older, we find there are fewer maps, fewer signs, and fewer people who can help us find our way.

It is easy to get sidetracked, confused and discouraged if we don't take time to slow down, and get clear. Fortunately, there is a method for examining and ranking the kinds of goals that make Life Plans work. The goals best suited to helping us move forward in our lives are SMART.

In other words, they are:

Specific
Measurable
Actionable
Realistic, and have a
Timeline

As your priorities become clear, it gets easier to say "yes" and "no" to new possibilities.

Empower

Who's got the power? You've got the power! This is a great slogan for a bumper sticker but, when it gets down to it, many times we feel like we don't have any power at all. We all get discouraged. We all have moments of doubt when we ask ourselves "What can I really do?" These feelings are an open invitation to worry and anxiety and there is already far too much worry and anxiety in the world.

To have power, and to be powerful, is to be connected, at a very deep level, to the knowledge and tools we need to live in the place and manner of our own choosing. Among the most dis-empowered people in America are people without housing who must struggle every day to find food and shelter. If you are fortunate enough to have food and shelter, it's time to empower yourself by gaining access to what you need to live the life you want. This is not a selfish act. Power, used wisely, is good. People you love need your power and people less fortunate than you can benefit from your power.

Ignite

When we accept the challenge of working toward a SMART goal, something changes inside of us. Putting ourselves "on the record" that we are going to make a change is a very big deal and leads us to stop wishing and start acting. Picking a goal, and working toward it, has been shown to reduce negative emotions and foster positive feelings about ourselves, and others. Experts in the field of human psychology have found that people who continue to focus on achieving specific goals also get better at sustaining those changes. These sparks can, and often do, ignite significant and unexpected personal growth.

Growth and change arrive together and the farther we progress on our journey toward the life we want to live, the more we need to learn. Personal growth requires continuous access to new and different knowledge and tools. When the poet Robert Browning wrote, "Ah, but a man's reach should exceed his grasp, or what's a heaven for?" he was reminding us it is noble to strive for a goal that isn't easily attainable. But this is not a summons to foolhardy behavior. Instead, Browning is giving us permission to practice perseverance in pursuit of success and accept defeat with grace and humility.

Measure

We begin making measurements at a very early age and don't stop until we take our last breath. The human eye can distinguish between 10 million colors. We can also detect minute differences in size and weight. Humans gather and use measurements all day, every day -- except when it comes to changing how we are living. It too often seems that satisfaction with life, or the lack thereof, is an entirely subjective thing. It isn't.

When we accept the challenge of creating a Life Plan, and have the conversations we need to have to discover what matters most to us, new possibilities begin to emerge. General feelings resolve into specific goals which can then be weighed, one against the other. When we know what we want, the things we need to be successful also come into focus. Every journey has its own, specific, requirements for knowledge, and tools.

Then comes the greatest question of all, "Am I moving closer to, or farther away from, my chosen destination?" This question cannot be answered without reliable measurements and every single measurement is a discovery in itself. This is how the great wheel of the Life Plan turns:

This is how we make a life worth living for ourselves, and for others.

Discover · Prioritize · Empower Ignite Measure

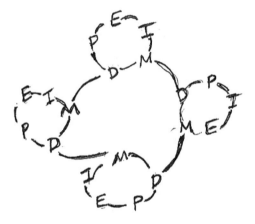

Afterword
Home is the Best Medicine

For more than a century, the hospital has occupied the center of the American healthcare system. Television shows like "Dr. Kildare," "St. Elsewhere," and "ER" taught generations of Americans that the best (and most attractive) doctors and nurses worked in (and seemingly never left) the hospital. Now, we are beginning to understand that while a hospital-centric health system might be good

for TV writers and great for people
with acute illnesses and injuries, it is
ill-suited to a world where most of the
care we provide is related to chronic
conditions.[32]

Change is mandatory because
national healthcare expenditures
are growing at an annual rate of 5.5
percent and are projected to reach
$5.7 trillion by 2026.[33] Spending on
hospitals currently totals $1.1 trillion
a year and consumes a third of total
health care costs.[34] Despite their un-
deniable high tech wizardry, hospitals
are less impressive when it comes to
caring for older people. A study by the
Office of the Inspector General of HHS
estimated that 13 percent of Medicare beneficiary hospitalizations had
adverse events that seriously harmed
these patients.[35]

The good news is we are now
moving away from a hospital-centric
fee-for-service-based "heads in beds"

system and towards value-based payments. By 2025 value-based care is expected to account for 100 percent of all Medicare payments and half of all Medicare and commercial insurance payments healthcare payments.[36] These changes are accelerating a decline in hospital utilization rates, especially for older people. Since the year 2000, per capita hospital admission rates for Medicare beneficiaries have fallen more than 25 percent.[37]

If home-centered health care seems like a strange new idea, it shouldn't. More than a century ago Florence Nightingale wrote: "Hospitals are only an intermediate stage of civilization, never intended, at all events, to take in the whole sick population." Instead, she hoped for the day when every "person will have the opportunity of a share in a district sick-nurse at home."[38] Joel Theisen, CEO of Minneapolis-based whole person senior services provider Lifesprk, is also a nurse and it's his mission to turn Nightingale's dream into a reality. "People talk about a health care system but what we actually have is a 'sick' care system. We need an alternative delivery system that addresses medical and social determinants of health."

The company's "life experience model" tracks data for every senior and has improved outcomes, reducing ER visits and hospitalizations by half. Instead of seeing older people in terms of deficits and diseases, Lifesprk concentrates on "sparking lives" and celebrates the value seniors bring to their families and communities. While national hospital readmission rates remain stubbornly high, 14.9 percent, this whole person approach to care has cut this rate in half.[39]

A home-based approach to health and well being must also contend with America's great housing mismatch. Currently, only 2 percent of American homes meet basic standards of accessibility essential to people living with mobility and cognitive challenges. The incidence of disability increases with age and almost half of Americans over the age of 75 do not have access to housing that meets their needs.[40] Big single family homes make life difficult for older people and this mismatch will become even more acute if, as Florence Nightingale predicted, health care is coming home.

This much is true, innovation is happening in the home and community. Alternatives must address everything that makes a person well long-term: transportation, access to quality care, focus on life and health goals, community resources, and more.

Lifesprk is building a scalable, whole person delivery system that is fearless in its pursuit to improve the life experience for seniors. By harnessing the power of big data and artificial intelligence, Lifesprk is creating its own powerful data platform, more intuitive than an EMR alone, capturing what matters most to seniors to drive multiple aims. We are partnering with payors and providers to help them get to value-based care and create the needed pathways to aggregate lives in a different way.

We're developing trusted, longitudinal, holistic, and deeply integrated relationships with those we serve, connecting them to everything they need to stay well.

Acknowledgements

This book springs from the work of the visionary architects of a true life experience alternative delivery system, Joel Thiesen and Carol Stanley. Their deep insights and un-yielding persistence created the LEADS model. This work was greatly im-proved by a dedicated group of skilled and compassionate experts in the field of supporting life-long independence who offered their stories, edits and invaluable commentary: Linda Brixius, Elisheva Carlson, Maren Christian-sen, Hilary Frank, Susan Garner, Michelle Gaulke, Sherlin Johnson, Shevon Olson, Candice Pautzke, Kelly Pritchard, Kari Schwartz and Kath-erine Swanson. John Berends, Amy Korzenowski and Allison O'Connor did the hard work of plowing through early drafts of this book helping it assume its present form. Sami Pelton put pen to paper and created the data drawings used in these pages and, importantly, kept this fast-moving publishing project on track. Kyrié Carpenter fused her deep knowledge of late life along with her eye for color and an ear for clarity of expression and turned a manuscript into the book you hold today. Finally, this has been a joyful collaboration with my spouse Jude Meyers Thomas. She poured her heart, soul, and considerable talent into the creation of the paintings that illustrate The Good Life.

Notes

1 https://nationalhealthcouncil.org/
   wp-content/uploads/2019/12/
   AboutChronicDisease.pdf
2 https://www.inc.com/amy-morin/
   americas-loneliness-epidemic-is-
   more-lethal-than-smoking-heres-
   what-you-can-do-to-combat-isola-
   tion.html
3 https://www.nia.nih.gov/news/
   social-isolation-loneliness-old-
   er-people-pose-health-risks#:~:-
   text=Health%20effects%20of%20
   social%20isolation,Alzheimer's%20
   disease%2C%20and%20even%20
   death.
4 https://www.cdc.gov/aging/publica-
   tions/features/lonely-older-adults.
   html
5 https://jamanetwork.com/
   journals/jamanetworkopen/fullarti-
   cle/2734064
6 https://www.sciencedirect.
   com/science/article/abs/pii/

S00223956616305441?via%3Dihub
7 Leo McCarey won Best Director for "The Awful Truth"
8 https://www.keiro.org/features/social-isolation-as-a-growing-epidemic
9 https://www.ncbi.nlm.nih.gov/pmc/articles/PMC4383762/
10 In order to avoid a 'response set' – where people give the same answer to a question almost by rote, it is important to alternate the direction of answers. E.g. for questions 1 and 3 you start with the 'Strongly Disagree' end of the scale and for question 2 you start with 'Strongly Agree'. Asking all three of these questions together produces the most reliable information results.
11 https://www.campaigntoendloneliness.org/wp-content/uploads/Loneliness-Measurement-Guidance1.pdf
12 https://www.ncoa.org/news/resources-for-reporters/get-the-facts/healthy-aging-facts/
13 Ward BW, Schiller JS, Goodman RA. Multiple Chronic Conditions Among US Adults: A 2012 Update. Prev

Chronic Dis 2014;11:130389.
14Int J Behav Nutr Phys Act. 2011 Jul 28;8:80. doi: 10.1186/1479-5868-8-80.
15https://www.rush.edu/health-wellness/discover-health/why-you-should-eat-breakfast
16https://www.ncbi.nlm.nih.gov/pubmed/15509817
17https://www.ncbi.nlm.nih.gov/pubmed/12421655
18https://newsinhealth.nih.gov/2013/04/benefits-slumber
19https://www.ncbi.nlm.nih.gov/pmc/articles/PMC5873393/#a-jag12491-bib-0001
20https://www.ncbi.nlm.nih.gov/pmc/articles/PMC5873393/#a-jag12491-bib-0004
21https://onlinelibrary.wiley.com/doi/pdf/10.1002/msj.20277
22https://money.cnn.com/2015/02/04/pf/money-stress/
23https://gerocentral.org/wp-content/uploads/2013/03/GAS-10-item-version-2015-1-15.pd\]
24https://www.alz.org/help-support/community/support-groups

25https://www.ncbi.nlm.nih.gov/pmc/
articles/PMC3487163/#:~:text=-
Schulz%20and%20Beach15%20
showed,years%20compared%20
to%20non%2Dcaregivers.

26http://nebula.wsimg.com/
f62738665d44b884416ddbffe0b-
872d0?AccessKeyId=954A289F7CD-
F75707C10&disposition=0&allowori-
gin=1

27Palmer, P. J. (2008). "The heart of
a teacher: Identity and integrity in
teaching" (PDF).

28https://www.frontiersin.org/arti-
cles/10.3389/fpsyg.2020.00151/full

29https://www.healthaffairs.org/doi/
full/10.1377/hlthaff.2017.0175

30https://jamanetwork.com/
journals/jamanetworkopen/fullarti-
cle/2734064

31https://www.sciencedirect.
com/science/article/abs/pii/
S0022395616305441?via%3Dihub

32https://www.statnews.
com/2018/05/31/chronic-diseas-
es-taxing-health-care-economy/

33https://www.cms.gov/
Research-Statistics-Data-and-Sys-

tems/Statistics-Trends-and-Reports/
NationalHealthExpendData/Down-
loads/ForecastSummary.pdf
34https://www.healthaf-
fairs.org/do/10.1377/
hblog20181206.671046/full/
35https://oig.hhs.gov/oei/reports/oei-
06-09-00090.pdf
36https://www.beckershospitalreview.
com/finance/new-goals-set-for-val-
ue-based-payments.html
37https://www.hcup-us.ahrq.gov/
reports/statbriefs/sb235-Inpatient-
Stays-Age-Payer-Trends.jsp
38Hospitals, dispensaries and nursing; papers and discussions in the
International congress of charities,
correction and philanthropy, section
III, Chicago, June 12th to 17th,
1893; 1894
39https://www.jchs.harvard.edu/re-
search-areas/aging
40https://www.statista.com/
statistics/240267/number-of-hous-
ing-units-in-the-united-states/

CPSIA information can be obtained
at www.ICGtesting.com
Printed in the USA
LVHW052148101121
702938LV00017B/1147